Shamanism for Beginners

The Ultimate Beginner's Guide to Walking the Path of the Shaman, Shamanic Journeying and Raising Consciousness

Your Free Gift (only available for a limited time)

Thanks for getting this book! If you want to learn more about various spirituality topics, then join Mari Silva's community and get a free guided meditation MP3 for awakening your third eye. This guided meditation mp3 is designed to open and strengthen ones third eye so you can experience a higher state of consciousness. Simply visit the link below the image to get started.

https://spiritualityspot.com/meditation

Contents

Introduction

Shamanism is not just an ancient healing tradition, but is also a way of life. It helps a shamanic practitioner connect with nature and the entire cosmic creation. Shamanic rituals are rooted in ancient spiritual practices of indigenous tribes all over the world. Although known by different names according to the language of each tribe, there is an uncanny number of similarities between various cultures of the globe separated by huge geographical differences.

These similarities indicate a strong connection between humans. It tells us that regardless of the culture or tribe we belong to, we all seek the same answers. The baffling questions of humankind remain the same which connect all of us to the same path. Most important, as you delve deep into Shamanism, you will notice a significant improvement in your ability to raise your levels of consciousness.

So, what differentiates this book from all the others? Well, for one, it is up-to-date and is written in very simple language. It is a great book for beginners, considering it has all the elements of shamanism explained from the perspective of a novice. You will not have to shift from book to book, trying to understand Shamanism's various concepts, but instead will find all the elements needed for a beginner within these pages, all for the cost of one book.

Let us start by understanding common terms used in Shamanism that will keep repeating throughout the book.

Cosmos - This refers to the entire universe which, according to Shamanism, is divided into three worlds, the Upper, Middle, and the Lower Worlds. The physical world that ordinary people experience is the ordinary aspect of the Middle World.

Two Realities - According to Shamanism, the ordinary state of consciousness (OSC) can access the ordinary aspects of the world. The shamanic state of consciousness (SSC) is required to access the extraordinary aspects of the cosmos.

Spirits - Spirits are beings living in all three Shamanic worlds. They are highly intelligent and empowered with amazing skills and knowledge.

Spirit Helpers or Guides - These are the beings of the spirit world who help and guide shamans during their shamanic journeys.

Shamanic Journeys - Shamans, in a shamanic state of consciousness (or altered state of consciousness), can undertake journeys using a part of their soul while their physical body remains in the physical world. In SSC, a shaman can perceive and experience non-ordinary spirits and realities.

Shamanic Tools - These are essential tools used by shamans for their work. The most common tools are the drum and the rattle used to induce an altered state of consciousness. Some shamans also use stones (crystals), wooden and metal objects, feathers, etc.

And finally, one of Shamanism's most important beliefs is that humans are not superior to other life forms. We all are interconnected with other life forms. Some of us have the power to speak to and interact with other life forms, including plants, animals, birds, etc.

So, don't hesitate. Get ahead and dive straight into the fascinating and marvelous world of Shamanism. The lessons in this book will help novices and beginners understand what Shamanism is all about and live a Shamanic life for improved self-awareness, raised consciousness, and increased personal and spiritual development.

Chapter 1: What is the Path of the Shaman?

Shamanism is an ancient religious practice involving a shaman, a practitioner with special powers to interact with the spirit world's beings through altered states of consciousness achieved through ecstatic religious experiences or trances. Frequently, shamans performed ritual rituals for interaction with spirits to allow them entry into the physical world to heal or for other purposes.

Scholars across various realms of learning, including history, archeology, anthropology, philosophy, psychology, and religion, are keenly interested in the concept of Shamanism and its varied uses. Hundreds of scholarly papers and research studies have been and continue to be conducted in Shamanism.

Interestingly, in the 20th century, Westerners standing up for counter-cultural movements have created a new, modern form of Shamanism called neo-shamanism consisting of many magic and religion-related practices influenced by their indigenous religions and cultures. Neo-Shamanism refers to new forms of this ancient practice used for healing and for seeing visions. Neo-Shamanism consists of an eclectic collection of ritualistic practices and belief systems based on achieving altered states of consciousness to communicate and connect with the world of spirits.

Neo-Shamanism is not a single cohesive system of belief. Instead, it is a collective term for multiple activities and philosophies primarily rooted in the belief in spiritual worlds. Thanks to indiscriminate practices by such people, the term Shamanism is treated with an undeserving mistrust and has suffered accusations and backlash regarding cultural appropriation.

In this book, we will focus on introducing important shamanic beliefs that have stood the test of time and have broken through the barriers built, wittingly or unwittingly, by followers of Neo-Shamanism.

The beliefs of ancient Shamanism, along with the connected rituals and practices, are primarily designed for us to connect with nature and to build self-awareness. Both these aspects are crucially helpful elements to the modern human world entangled and embroiled in the relentless rat race of life.

The word Shamanism is believed to have been derived from "saman", a Manchu-Tungu word that means "one who knows." Manchu-Tungus belongs to a group of languages collectively called Tungusic and is spoken in Manchuria and Eastern Siberia. According to another version, the word may have its origins in the Evenki (another Tungusic language) word "saman".

Many of these tongues are on the verge of extinction today. The Tungusic phrase is recorded in the memoirs of Avvakum, an exiled Russian clergyman. The term has been adopted by the Russians who interacted with the indigenous Siberian tribes.

Shamanism was introduced to Western Europe in the last 17th century. In 1692, Nicolaes Witsen, a Dutch traveler, published a book titled "Noord en Oost Tataryen" based on his experiences with the Tungusic-speaking indigenous tribes of Siberia. Again, in 1968, Adam Branch, a German merchant, published a book that describes his account of a Russian embassy to China. In the same year, an English translation of this book introduced Shamanism to the English-speaking world.

What is the definition of Shamanism? Anthropologists define Shamanism in various ways. There is not a single definition that can embrace everything this fascinating topic stands for. One definition goes like this, "*A shaman is one who can connect with the spirit world while he or she is in an altered state of consciousness.*"

Another definition is the same as above, except that the shaman would contact the spirit world only at the behest of someone else. A third definition tries to differentiate a shaman from the magico-religious specialists like witch-doctors, mediums, prophets, spiritual healers, etc. This differentiation definition claims that a shaman uses unique techniques not known or used by the other pseudo practitioners. We can say that shamans are those who have access to and influence in the spirit world and practice divination and healing through trance-inducing rituals.

To end this section, it might make sense to recall the definition of a shaman as described by Christina Pratt in her book, "An Encyclopedia of Shamanism." According to this definition, a shaman has mastered three elements, namely:

- How to achieve altered states of consciousness.

- How to act as a mediator between the physical and spirit worlds to be useful to the community.

- To meet the needs of a doctor, psychiatrist, and religious leaders in the tribe.

History of Shamanism

Shamanism has historically been associated with tribal and indigenous societies that believed in a shaman's power to connect with the spirit world. Shamans have been using this power to perform miracles for the people in the living world to heal the sick, solve problems left behind by the dead people, and even escort the souls of the dead to the afterlife.

According to many recorded historical ethnographies, shamans were male, female, transgender, and all ages starting from adolescence. Shamanism ideology has been and continues to be practiced widely in many parts of the world, including Asia, Europe, North and South America, Tibet, and Africa. As seen from the previous paragraphs, the underlying concept was the belief in supernatural phenomena like the world of demons, gods, spirits, and other-worldly beings with the power to do good for humans.

Most experts agree that Shamanism is likely to have originated among the hunter-gatherers of prehistoric times and persisted within certain farming and herding tribes after the growth and spread of agriculture. Historians, anthropologists, and other experts agree that the primary concept originated among the indigenous Siberian tribes who would gather a highly psychoactive (sometimes even poisonous) mushroom, Amanita muscaria.

Unfortunately, Shamans have been the target of many social and political powers that have tried to suppress the practice of traditional spiritual rituals based on ancient beliefs, primarily driven by differing opinions and cultures. Despite these attacks, many tribal communities have kept their traditions alive and there has been a resurgence supported by a deep faith in these tried and tested old belief systems. Numerous tribes have stood up and fought against suppressions by cultures that differ from their own. They are trying to reclaim their dynamic traditions, regardless of the beliefs and faiths of others.

Interestingly, a few of the tribal groups have unwittingly kept themselves aloof from modern influences because of them being isolated from the effects of threatening social, political, and cultural impediments. For example, the nomadic tribe called Tuvans (their global population is a mere 3,000) have survived the cruel onslaught of modernization and sometimes deliberate structural impediments. Tuva is one of Russia's most isolated tribes, where Shamanism has remained untouched and free from the influences of other religions.

The initiation and learning of Shamanism is purely a matter of personal calling. The calling to become a shaman can come through dreams or signs. Also, some shamans inherit this power from their parents, grandparents, etc. Generally, the training to become a shaman takes years, although the time varies depending on the community and the powers of the concerned individual.

Kevin Turner, MA, a scholar, and shaman who has dedicated his life to Shamanism, talks about a rite of passage that all potential shamans must go through. He calls this rite of passage a "shamanistic initiatory crisis," and it involves a psychological crisis or a physical illness. This "initial crisis" element plays a huge role in the personal calling experience of an individual.

The "wounded healer" is an archetypal reference to the start of a shamanic journey. This sickness or crisis, particularly important for young potentials, involves a state wherein the individual reaches the brink of death, which helps him or her in these ways:

- The shaman breaches the line separating the world of the living from the spiritual world, crosses over, ventures into the other side, and brings back important information for the human world.

- A shaman must become sick to understand sickness. Only when a novitiate overcomes the illness will he or she have the power to hold the cure to heal others' sufferings.

Most shamans get messages from the spirit world through signs, visions, or dreams. Some shamans have spirit guides who help and guide the shaman's journeys to the spiritual world. A few of the spirit guides are believed to reside in the body of the shaman, but some spirit guides can be accessed only when the shaman is in a trance.

During the trance, the spirit guide energizes the shaman, empowering him or her to enter the world of spirits and guide them through the journey. Shamans return to the world of living with the lost parts of the soul of the sufferers, which help to heal the affected people. Also, shamans have the power to eliminate and cleanse negative energies that pollute and confuse the souls of the sufferers.

Shamans also act as mediators between the living and spiritual world. With the power to communicate with both realms, they help to reduce unrest, resolve unsettled issues, and deliver gifts and offerings from the living world to the spirits.

Animal Symbolism in Shamanism

Shamanism is often syncretic with animism, which is rooted in belief systems wherein the world is home to multiple spirit-worlds and spirit beings with the power to help or hinder humankind's endeavors. So, you can see a lot of animal symbolism in Shamanism. Each tribe had a spirit animal of its own. For example, for the Selkups, a native tribe of Northern Siberia, the spirit animal was the sea duck. Considering that the sea duck can fly in the air and dive in the water, the Selkups believe that it belongs to the upper and lower worlds. For the same reason, waterfowl are seen as spirit animals for other Siberian tribes.

Shamanism believes that the upper world is the afterlife, a world connected with deceased people. The upper world can be accessed through a portal in the sky by traveling souls of the dead. The lower world is the afterlife of animals and can be accessed through a portal on the surface of the earth. Many animals, therefore, are treated as animal spirits.

The duties of shamans include:

- Healing

- Leading a sacrifice

- Narrating songs and telling stories to preserve traditions and culture

- Fortune-telling

- Guiding souls to the afterlife

A few shamans can do all these duties, but not all are well-versed in all the functions listed above. Guiding of souls can happen individually or in a group, again depending on the culture of the tribe. Shamans can cure both physical and mental afflictions. They also perform and spirit-exhorting rituals.

Classic Shamanism, a term used to refer to Shamanism practiced in North Asia in the 19th century, has clearly defined tenets and traits of the religion and shamans. Some of these characteristics include:

The concerned community accepts there are people among themselves with special powers to communicate with the transcendental world. These special individuals can heal physical and mental sickness and do other extraordinary activities beyond the average person.

Shamans have eccentric personalities and are also known for special mental traits, including being highly intuitive, mercurial, and sensitive. Also, shamans could have a physical defect such as an extra toe or finger, lameness, and extra teeth.

A shaman becomes one not only because of his or her calling to the cause of Shamanism but also because of persistent follow-up by supernatural beings with the final say in making shamans out of ordinary individuals. Most often, potential shamans get their calling during their adolescent years, but most are likely to resist the calling for years.

The supernatural being connected to this shaman uses various forms of torture like physical and mental illnesses to break the resistance of the candidate until the person is left with no choice but to become a shaman.

A few types of shamans are trained for specialized rituals and functions. For instance, among the Nanai, a Tungusic tribe of Far East Russia and East Asia, only an approved shaman distinctively trained can be a psychopomp (someone who guides souls to the afterlife). Similarly, the Selkup, Enet, and Nenet tribes have their own specialized shamans for specific interactions with the spirit world.

A shaman is always accompanied by an assistant called Oroqen shaman (or the second spirit). This second shaman participates in the shamanic rituals and interprets the primary shaman's actions and behaviors, who would be in a trance, but this second shaman (also called the jardalanin) is not acting as an actual shaman, and he or she should not fall into a trance state.

Shamanism and Ecological Preservation

The Tucano tribe, an indigenous group in South America, uses a highly sophisticated system to preserve their environment and ecology and avoid depleting resources because of overhunting. Keeping overhunting in check and preserving the balance of nature is rooted in mythological beliefs. According to these belief systems, people who break hunting restrictions can become seriously ill!

It is easily open to conjecture that shamans are likely to have participated in laying down the foundations of such a system by actively restricting excessive fishing and hunting. Perhaps, he or she demonstrated powers to "release" the souls of animals from their abode to cause sickness, the fear of which could have been a way to discourage people from indulging in excesses. Similar Shamanism-driven approaches for balancing and preserving nature are taken by the Piaroa tribe (in present-day Venezuela), Inuit tribe, and others.

The next question is, "Do shamans make money? If yes, how?" Shamans get their sustenance as they conduct and participate in the everyday rituals of the tribe they belong to. They provide ritualistic services and get paid for it. The belief is that the payment goes on to the helpful spirit that came in handy to solve the problem.

The goods and payments received by the spirit are given back to the shaman because they need to use the profits thus received to continue their regular work, but it is also important to note that these gifts and money received while performing rituals are only additional income. Most often, shamans lead their lives like the other tribes in his or her community, as hunters, farmers, cattle-rearers, etc. Women shamans are also housewives.

The path of a shaman and the aspects of Shamanism are summarized below:

- Spirits and their world exist, and both play a significant role in our personal and social lives.

- Shamans have the power to communicate and interact with the spirit world.

- There are both bad and good spirits.

- Shamans can heal illnesses caused by evil or bad spirits.

- Shamans use trance states to incite visions and go on journeys to the spirit world. The shaman's spirit goes into the spirit world while the physical body appears to be in a trance.

- Shamans use the energy of spirit guides and animal symbolism for their rituals.

Contemporary Shamanism

Dr. Michael Harner, an American professor of anthropology, is credited with having popularized and established contemporary Shamanism. He taught shamanic healing practices and rituals to Westerners in the early 1970s. Until then, the concept was not well-known outside the world of academia.

Modern-day shamans are commonly called "shamanic practitioners." You can find them throughout Europe and the US. Many owe their education and learning of Shamanism to Dr. Michael Harner and his non-profit organization, Foundation for Shamanic Studies (FSS), which began in 1985. His famous book, "The Way of the Shaman," is a pioneer in contemporary shamanism.

Now that you understand Shamanism and shamans, we can look at who can become a shaman in the next chapter.

Chapter 2: Who Can Walk the Path?

Shamanism is practiced in multiple geographies across the world, including many parts of Asia, Europe, North and South America, the Oceania regions, and Africa. The last chapter had details of Shamanism practiced by the natives of Russia and Siberia. Let us look at the other regions and see how a shaman candidate is chosen and trained.

Shamanism in Japan - Shamanism is deeply embedded in Japan's ancient local religions, namely Shintoism and Ainu, both of which are also rooted in animism. At the start of the Middle Ages, Japanese beliefs began to be influenced by Buddhism, and since then, a lot of syntheses have taken place between the two belief systems and, today, a syncretized version of Shamanism, Shintoism, and Buddhism is prevalent across this highly developed Asian nation.

Shamanism in China - China is one of the oldest civilizations in the world. Even today, the Hmong tribe, which has a 5000-year-old history, continues to practice its own form of Shamanism known as Ua Neeb.

A Hmong shaman's primary task is to maintain harmony and balance in the community by helping individuals and families find balance and harmony. The Hmong shamans also perform trance-driven rituals for environmental harmony. About 200,000 Hmong people re-settled in the US after the Vietnam War. Even today, Shamanism is a huge part of the Hmong settlers in the US.

The Hmong people's shamanic practices include animal sacrifices, which are conducted with a lot of respect and care. According to Hmong beliefs, everything in this world has a soul (sometimes, even multiple souls). All the souls are treated as equal and are interchangeable. A person becomes sick because his or her soul gets lost or captured by a wild spirit. A chosen animal's (it could be a pig, chicken, dog, goat, etc.) approval or permission must cure such an afflicted person.

The ritual involves exchanging the animal's soul for the soul of the afflicted person for 12 months. At the end of the 12 months, the chosen animal is sacrificed with great respect, its soul sent to the spirit world as promised. The souls of animals so sacrificed are believed to be reborn as a higher form of a living being. Such souls could also become a member of a god's family to live a life free of suffering. So, it is believed that animals who get chosen for sacrifice by shamans are honored creatures because they get to be of service to mankind and get a better life than now.

Physical sickness is also cured using sacred words called "khawv koob."

Shamanism in Malaysia – a few of the indigenous tribes of Malaysia, including those living Sabah and Sarawak regions, practice a form of Shamanism, which they call pawang or bomoh. In the Sabah region, the primary shaman is called Bobohizan or Bobolian, the high priest or priestess.

Shamanism in Korea - Shamanism is still prevalent in both North and South Korea. In South Korea, female shamans are called mudangs, and male shamans are called baksoo mudangs. An individual can become a shaman through a hereditary title or personal calling and natural abilities. In modern times, shamans are consulted for resolving financial and marital problems.

Shamanism in the Philippines - Shamanism was practiced in the pre-colonial Philippines among many tribes. The name given to shamans in this region was Babaylans or balian or katalonan, and most often, these shamans were female. The shamans of the Philippine islands were specialized in harnessing nature's power for humankind.

Spirit guides helped Babaylans contact, communicate, and interact with the spirit world's spirits and deities. Deities of the spirit world were called diwata or anito. Shamans were primarily mediums at seance rituals. Different types of shamans specialized in various functions, including healing, divination, sorcery, and herbalism.

Babaylans were highly respected and were on a par with the noble class of those times. Absent the head of a tribe, a Babaylan donned an interim head's role. They were powerful performers of rituals and rites needed to influence nature, including affecting climate and weather and harnessing nature's various spirits.

Babaylans could counter dark magic used by evil spirits. Besides healing the sick, the Babaylans were empowered to ensure safe pregnancy and childbirth. Also, they led all rituals dealing with offerings to various gods and goddesses. Well-versed in herbs, they knew how to create curing potions, remedies, and antidotes using seeds, roots, and leaves of plants.

These rituals and rites and the influence of Babaylans declined when Islam reached the Philippines, and most of the ethnic groups of the country were converted. Also, under the Spanish Empire, Babaylans were maligned as evil witches and were persecuted mercilessly. Numerous Shamanic symbols, shrines, and ritualistic materials were burned down.

Today, the Philippine society's shamans are called folk healers and are mostly men. Some women shamans are still accused of witchcraft. For the indigenous people belonging to the areas that remained out of Spanish and Islamic influence, Shamanism continues to be practiced, although in a highly diluted form.

Shamanism in Mongolia - The oldest surviving literary work in the Mongolian language is "The Secret History of the Mongols," written in the 13th century for the Mongol royal family after the death of Ghengis Khan. This classic explains male and female shamans working as healers, exorcists, soothsayers, rainmakers, and even officials in the royal court of clan-based Mongolian society.

The spiritual hierarchy was layered and complex. The highest spiritual group consisted of 99 tngri (or divinities) and 77 natigai or *earth mothers*. The group of 99 tngri common to all the clans in Mongolia consisted of 55 benevolent or white tngri and 44 black or terrifying divinities. These were called upon only by great shamans and leaders.

The next level of spirits were three groups of ancestral spirits called Lord-Spirits, Protector-Spirits, and Guardian-Spirits. The Lord-Spirits consisted of the souls of dead clan leaders. Any clan member can contact the Lord-Spirits and appeal for spiritual and physical help.

The Protector-Spirits consisted of the souls of great male and female shamans who were called jigari and abjiya, respectively, in the Mongolian language. The Guardian-Spirits were the souls of smaller male and female shamans (boge and idugan, respectively). These were associated with a specific neighborhood, location, or geographical forms such as rivers and mountains, within a particular clan's territory.

In the 1990s, a modern approach was given to Mongolian Shamanism, resulting in a new form of Mongolian Neo-Shamanism. During this time, there was a proliferation of shamans among the

Buryat Mongols living in Russia and Mongolia. This proliferation, combined with the advent of the Mongolian Neo-Shamanism, gave the Buryats the impetus to fight for the re-establishment of their genetic and historical roots in the region.

Interestingly, many Mongolian shamans today have turned Shamanic practices into a business and have large offices in towns and cities, but in these office premises, too, shamans perform the services of healing, resolving physical and mental problems, and fortune-telling. Shamanic practices continue even in modern times in Mongolian culture, although many shamans have taken on a wary approach to Neo-Shamanism.

Shamanism in the Polar regions - Eskimo tribes and groups occupy a large area covering eastern Siberia and going through Alaska. Northern Canada and Greenland. Shamanic practices and rituals have been recorded among many of these tribes cutting across continental borders. Shamans are also mediators, as you already know. The role of mediators in Eskimo groups is well known, and mediators are believed to have the power to connect with the spirit world.

Shamanism in North America - Native Americans did not have one universal religious system or belief. There are over 550 Native American tribes in the US and over 600 First Nations tribes in Canada. Native American tribes had singers, healers, lore-keepers, mystics, fortune-tellers, medicine-men, and other shaman-like duties. But the word shaman was never used to describe them. Each tribe described such people in its own language.

Unfortunately, with the Americas' colonial occupation, practicing religious rituals and sacred ceremonies was made illegal until 1978, when the American Indian Religious Freedom Act was passed, but the traditional rituals and ceremonies were not forgotten by the Native Americans. They just went underground and were practiced secretly until the repressive laws were repealed. Shamans in North America usually get their position and power through a personal quest, inheritance, spiritual calling, or elections.

Shamanism in Africa - In the African continent, too, each tribe had its own set of healing and divination functionaries. For example, in Mali, the Dogon sorcerers, who could be male or female, communicate with a spirit named Amma. Amma is believed to advise on divination and healing practices.

Shamanism in South America - Shamanism in South America is prevalent mostly in the Amazonian region. The shamans here are similar to tribal chiefs in terms of power and position. The shamans of South America are closely connected to jaguars. The shamans are believed to have the power to transform jaguars at will. Jaguars are not considered real animals, but a transformed living shaman or the spirit of a dead shaman traveling through the physical world.

Shamans in South America depend mostly on Ayahuasca to achieve the trance state. Today, the scientific world knows how this psychoactive plant works, but it is still a mystery how the ancient shamans knew how and in what proportion to use this element to induce the perfect trance-like state.

Also, rattles instead of drums are used to induce a trance state. The rattle's gourd is believed to represent the universe, and the stones or seeds inside it signifies the souls of ancestors. The connection between the shaman and the souls inside the rattle happens through the handle, which is seen as a pathway or portal to connect to the cosmos.

The Significance of Shamanic Rituals

A key feature of shamanic rituals is that they are religious ceremonies and artistic performances, but the point to note is that the drama surrounding the rituals is not to create any spectacle or to draw undue attention, but to lead the community in a solemn ceremony.

There are four elements in any shamanic ceremony, namely music, dance, poetry, and mimetic drama. A Shaman uses these elements outwardly to manifest and express his or her mystical communication with the spirit world so the rest of the community can see it. A true shaman can also communicate with the spirit world through his or her guardian spirit anytime, anywhere. These rituals are a way of demonstrating their power to the tribe so everyone in the community can also partake and share the shaman's religious experience.

The shaman leading the ritual changes his or her voice mimetically to represent the spirits and divine beings he or she encounters and interacts with in the journey to the spirit world. Shamans practice ventriloquism and even learn to mimic animal sounds and nature's elements to recreate a magical experience for their audience. The dances and music and songs make the spiritual adventure a living reality for the tribe's people.

Although the costumes of the shamans vary across different tribes, the common accessories include a drum or tambourine, a cap, and a coat. Changing into animal shapes form a crucial aspect of journeying into the spirit world, so the coat and cap are decorated with heads, feathers, and furs of chosen animals.

The tambourine or drum, which represents the universe, is used to communicate with the spirits even as the sound enables the shaman to achieve altered states of consciousness. The drum is also divided into equal halves to represent lower realms and the earth. Natural objects and symbols are added to the instrument to represent heavenly bodies and natural forces.

The well-being and health of the entire community, including the people, plants, animals, and the surrounding environment, are the responsibility of a shaman. They travel to the spirit world by inducing a state of trance that results in spiritual, emotional, and even physical transformations. Shamans achieve this trance state through various methods depending on the customs and traditions of the culture and community they belong to.

Healers of the Native American tribes achieve the state of trance using deprivation techniques like isolation and fasting. Shamans from South America and Siberia use intoxicants and hallucinogens like peyote, alcohol, mushrooms, and Ayahuasca (a tea made from a psychoactive plant).

Roles of a Shaman

We looked at the roles that a shaman fits into briefly. Let us look at these roles in detail and see how each role's functions are used.

Healers - Shamans in their state of trance heal the sick by entering the body of the sick person to confront the illness-causing spirit. They banish the infectious spirit resulting in healing. Also, sometimes, they heal a part of the affected person's soul by repairing the part. And shamans know of herbs and plant life in their area, empowering them to use herbal remedies to heal and cure sicknesses.

Mediators - As mediators, shamans communicate with the spirit world and exchange messages between the physical and spiritual realms. Also, their mediating and negotiating skills come in handy to resolve differences between the ordinary members of the tribe and religious entities. In certain tribes, shamans play the role of various diviners such as soothsayers and palm readers.

Miscellaneous Roles - The shamans from the Siberian tribes have great power and control over spirits. They can prevent spirits from causing harm to the people of their community. Sometimes, shamans serve as mediums for spirits who want to communicate with the people in the physical realm.

Whatever their specific roles may be, the primary role of a shaman is to maintain harmony in the community. They are caretakers of the traditional culture of their community. Their years of experience dealing with people and spirits make them ideal candidates for counselors and advisors.

The next logical question is, "Can an average, ordinary person in the modern world become a shaman?" Now that shamanism is getting a revival of sorts, this question is valid that needs attention. The wise shamans of yore believed and accepted that the material world is a manifestation of realms of subtle energies, and certain people with certain skillsets can access these subtle energy layers.

In a paper by Marlene Dobkin de Rios, Ph.D., published in the American Journal of Public Health in 2002, she says that practicing shamanic rituals can be useful to develop their power, to make positive behavioral changes, both of which can help them cope with emotional, psychological, and physical issues, but it is important to note that there is not a single approved institution that trains or registers shamanic practitioners and healers.

So, ordinary people like you and I can walk the path of Shamanism by harnessing the power of intuition and self-awareness. As you walk the path, you will notice a slow but sure growth in your personal development and your instinctive abilities. With access to this improved personal power, you can build a harmonious relationship with the world around you, even as they help you improve self-awareness significantly.

In the next chapter, you can learn various tips and tricks to make a personal shamanic journey and to harness its benefits.

Chapter 3: Building a Shamanic Life

Building a Shamanic way of life is in your own hands. With the right mindset, by diligently following daily routines and a few changes in your daily habits, you can see the sacred and beauty in the mundane. Let us get right into journey work.

So, what are journeys in the world of Shamanism? A shaman's most important task is to undertake journeys into the spirit world. Journeying is one of the most common and essential tools used by a shaman. The best thing about journeys in Shamanism is that they can be done in conjunction with any belief system. You would not need to give up your current faith to undertake Shamanism journey work.

Drums play an important role in journeys. The drumbeat's monotonous rhythm impacts the theta waves in your brain, which alters the perception of reality, so you go into a state of trance or the journey state.

Journeying is theoretically straightforward, but it is a challenge to learn and master it. It will be a challenge for novices. The trick is in diligent, persistent practice. The more you practice the shamanic journey, the more you will discover. Here are a few tips to get started, and then we will go into some elements later. You will need these elements, to begin with:

- A quiet, undisturbed place and time where you can lay down comfortably.

- A cloth or cover to close your eyes.

- The sound of a drumbeat. You could use any drumming tracks available freely on the internet if you don't have your own drummer.

Getting into an altered state is a difficult thing to achieve. And once you reach that state, being disturbed in the middle of your journey will break your trance and leave you feeling disoriented. So, taking care you will not be disturbed through the duration of your shamanic journey is critical. For example, if you have pets, then make sure they are out of your chosen spot.

The drumbeat is typically very monotonous. The monotony and boredom of the drumming rhythm should be such that it should not engage with your conscious mind. If you allow your conscious mind to be engaged in great music, then your subconscious mind cannot venture into the spirit world.

Another important reason for the drumming to be monotonously rhythmic is that it is effective during the call back when there should be a distinct shift in the rhythm triggering your journey back into the physical world. The callback rhythm shifts from the monotonous beat to a complete stop. Then, there are four sets of seven beats, after which comes a series of disjointed drumming beats. The entire call back duration lasts about one to two minutes, which is enough time for you to return from the spirit world to the physical world. Here are a few tips to follow when you return:

- First, you are likely to feel a little disoriented. The best way to ride over this feeling is by wiggling your toes and fingers, licking your lips, and engaging in simple gestures and activities that will help you re-engage with the physical world.

- Pat your body all over and make sure you feel fully aware of your surroundings.

- If you still feel a little dizzy or disoriented, say your name out loud three to four times. Hearing the sound of your name in your voice helps you re-engage with the three-dimensional real world in which you need to live and function.

- Each time you undertake a journey and return, record your experiences and all the details you can remember.

Now that you have a general idea of what to expect in your shamanic journey, let us get down to the details of a few important elements.

Finding Your Anchor Spot

Finding your anchor spot is the first step you should take on your path to building a shamanic life. So, what is the anchor spot? It is the starting place of your journey. It is a safe spot you are comfortable and familiar with. You will need this anchor spot right through your journey. The deeper and more complex your shamanic practices become, the more important your anchor spot becomes. The anchor spot is a Middle World Journey. The Three Shamanic Worlds are discussed in a later chapter.

The anchor spot is where you start all your shamanic travels, at least in the initial days of learning. Many experienced shamans use their anchor spot even after years of practice. This spot is what you will picture when the drum starts to beat. This picture reflects a safe spot where you feel secure.

Choosing an anchor spot is entirely a personal choice. It could be a favorite park in your neighborhood you have visited often. It could be your backyard or garden where you enjoy spending time with your plants. It could be your favorite beach where you smell the enticing air, watch and hear the waves breaking over the rocks, and hear the seagulls mewing as they fly over the unending blue waters of the ocean.

The trick is to engage deeply with your mind and imagination so this picture or anchor spot is embedded deep inside your psyche. When the drum starts beating, you immediately see this place in nature from where you can start your journey. When you start your first journey, don't think about the travel. Just focus on the anchor spot.

Look around you. What do you see? Trees? Meadows? Can you spot any characteristic feature of the picture? Turn your eyes and body all around and see in all the directions from that spot. Walk a few steps in each direction and make mental notes of what you see, hear, and feel.

Your anchor spot will become the doorway into the spirit world, so you must spend time in the initial few days of initiation on the anchor spot and make it a part of your spiritual world.

Meditation to find your anchor spot - Undertaking shamanic journeys, including finding your anchor spot, takes a lot of practice, and getting it right will require time and effort. If meditation-driven visualizations are suitable for you, then you can use this tool, which can be a great bridge to cover the distance between meditation and beginning your shamanic journey.

For the novice, meditation is a practice involving the training of your mind to induce a shift in consciousness. Meditation can be done either for benefit or merely to identify and acknowledge the wondrous experience of discovering new planes of consciousness. As you meditate, focus on your chosen anchor spot, and make mental notes of all the details you sense, including the sounds, smells, sights, etc.

Meditation is a great tool to reduce the difficulty in finding and identifying your anchor spot.

Finding Your Power Animals

Your power animal can be any animal, being, or natural object that stands and symbolizes a specific type of energy. Awakening and honoring the spirit of your power animal will release the mystical, spiritual energies into your life as a shaman. So, why an animal? You might want to ask this. Read on to discover why shamans have power animals they connect to.

Our ancestors watched animals carefully. They observed animal behaviors, traits, habits, and their sharp abilities to survive and thrive in the wilderness. Shaman ancestors especially did this activity because they could connect with all life forms, including animals – thanks to their enhanced senses.

These wise shamans of yore used mythical lore to tell and retell their observations of spiritual animals as they traveled through the spirit world. These shamans noted similarities between earth animals and spirit animals and noted similarities in traits and habits. All power animals need not have earthly manifestations because they are not bound by physical form.

So, every shaman can have any power animal, and you need not be restricted by any number either. For example, in your early days, you could use a deer as a power animal, but as you delve deep into your journey, your power animal could change into something else, with or without an earthly manifestation. Also, remember that power animals are not worshipped. They are only followed, and shamans harness their energies.

Your power animal will share a lot of information with you as you undertake the shamanic journey through dreams and visions. Your power animal is something you aspire to be, even as you try to live according to a code of honor set by it. The reason animal and human lives are so entwined is that we have a lot to learn from each other. So, animals come to us on their own accord because they have a lesson to pass on or want to learn something from us.

Power animals seek to offer us love, understanding, knowledge, and energy, which are highly useful elements in the path of a shamanic journey. So, how do you find your power animal? Here are a few tips to help you get started:

Start the drumbeat sound and allow your body to relax in a quiet, undisturbed place.

Set your intention, a critical step in any spirit-related work. The best way to do this is by saying out loud, "I am on my journey to find my power animal."

Close your eyes as your body relaxes and visualize your anchor spot. This will be your entry point into the lower world to find your power animal.

The portal that allows you entry into the lower world could be a foxhole, a hollow in a big tree trunk, a crater at the top of a tree stump, a waterfall, a ladder, or anything else that will help you climb down into the lower world. Also, find something at the entry point that can lead you down an elevator or a step ladder.

A crucial piece of advice at this time is that the point of entry into the lower world will not be very comfortable, especially in the initial days of your journeying work. For example, it will be a difficult task for an average person to fit into a foxhole and climb down, right? This logic holds good in the spirit world, but once you have made up your mind, then you can fit into any portal of your choice regardless of the apparent discomfort.

Don't get overwhelmed by the difficulty and give up. The spirits are likely using it as a way of testing your resilience and determination to become a shaman. The ability to overcome your discomfort and pain will be your gift from the spirit world, a sign you have been accepted there.

When you have passed through the entrance and entered the world of spirits, be ready to accept whatever you see. The sight in front of you could be a wondrous setting in the depths of an overgrown, green forest. It could be a beach with the setting sun sending splendorous-colored evening rays across the sky. It could be a simple walking path flanked by tall, dark trees or a spectacular cave of crystals. Just accept whatever you see when you enter and revel in the scenery.

Your next job is to wait at this entrance for your power animal to come to you. Shamanism believes that whatever and whoever has to find you will do so on their own. As shamans, we only need to be patient and wait for things to happen to us. The lower world is not a dangerous place you must fear. Wait until your power animal finds you.

So, how do you know when you see your power animal? Well, traditionally, we suggest that if you see an animal appear four times before you while you wait at the entrance, then it is your power animal, but more important, as a novice shaman, your intuitive powers will be strong enough for you to realize what your power animal is.

Another way of seeking a power animal is to question the animal, "Are you my power animal?" Many animals reply verbally, telepathically, or even mime out their responses to seekers. And interestingly, some animals might even reply to your question in the negative. Don't be disappointed. All you have to do is to wait until your power animal appears.

You may fail in finding your power animal in your first journey to the lower world. Don't be discouraged by the apparent failure. Most shamans do not find their power animal on the first journey itself. Another important tip is not to set your heart out on any particular animal or species of animal. Just empty your mind and wait for the right one to find you.

No power animal is more powerful than another. Every animal has its set of unique traits, and it partners with you because you need its power and traits. You are likely to be surprised by the animal that finds you eventually and becomes your power animal. An important piece of advice at this stage is not to venture far from the entrance to the lower world without your power animal. Although this part of the world is not dangerous, it is unfamiliar for novices, and you could get lost.

Once you find your power animal, then you can freely access the lower world. Just remember to stay close to your guiding animal as you can get directionally challenged in the unfamiliar territory. Also, when you hear your call back signal, you might not find your way back to the entrance. But you need not worry because your power animal will help you get to the doorway with plenty of time to space.

Knowing the Four Directions Through the Medicine Wheel

The Medicine Wheel is a representation of the four directions east, west, north, and south, and has been used for centuries by different tribes for various purposes. It is an important symbol in Shamanism and stands for the harmonious relationship existing among all living beings on Earth. Medicine Wheels across the globe employ a varied range of colors and animal symbols and totems.

The directions depicted by the Medicine Wheel stand for different aspects of the human and spirit worlds. Here is a small summary for each of the four directions and the elements it depicts on the Medicine Wheel:

> • **North** - North stands for night, afterlife, the earth element, and the spiritual aspect of human life. The animals connected with the north are buffalo and celestial animals.

- **East** - This direction stands for dawn, birth, the air element, and the human's mental state. The East direction represents deer, hawk, and eagle.

- **South** - The southern direction stands for mid-day, life, the fire element, and the human's physical state. The animals represented by the South are coyotes, foxes, and lions.

- **West** - The western direction stands for dusk, death, the water element, and the human's emotional state. The animals connected with the western direction are the bear and jaguar.

The Medicine Wheel has changed its form multiple times to suit the needs of each tribe. It has also moved from being a community tool to becoming a thing of personal connection for everyone. As its name suggests, the Wheel has adapted, moved, and has fit itself in useful and productive ways in the world of Shamanism, helping shamans heal themselves, their community, and the world. The next chapter deals with the Medicine Wheel and the Four Directions in the world of Shamanism.

Chapter 4: The Medicine Wheel and the Four Directions

Studying the Medicine Wheel is a paradox of sorts. It is simple yet complicated in its own way. The factors that affect the representation of the wheels include geographical location, cosmology, shamans, and priests working with it, and concepts of sacred geometry. As our learning increases, so do our perceptions and understanding of the wheel. We learn and develop as we pass through the sections of the wheel. The center of this fascinating wheel is the spirit or the pure heart or the final truth. Everything else extends from the center, and also, everything converges into the center.

When you see a diagram or photo of a Medicine Wheel, it is two-dimensional, right? But when shaman ancestors created a wheel, they made sure it represented all aspects of nature, the human world, and the invisible elements of the universe. The rhythm of life supports the Medicine Wheel.

Humans have been and continue to learn from observing nature. Shamanism's core principle is that the world and a lot of things in nature form a circle. For example, the earth is a circle; the tree trunk is a circle, bird nests are usually a circle, water droplets are circular, the seasons happen in a circle, and more. Most of the world around you expresses itself in circular patterns.

The Medicine Wheel demonstrates that everything in this world is interconnected, and in turn, everything is linked to the cosmic center. The Medicine Wheel is a manifestation of our spiritual energy and our internal dialogue. It acts as a mirror to help us improve our understanding of what is going on within us. It is also a wheel of protection, enabling us to collect all the surrounding energies into a focal point so we can communicate with the spirit. Let's try to explain this fascinating and crucial aspect of Shamanism in a bit of detail in this chapter dedicated to it.

Understanding the Medicine Wheel

Medicine wheels are also known as hoops, and as already mentioned, its uses and purposes are specific to a culture, but different the culture-specific elements may be, one fundamental similarity connects all forms of the Medicine Wheel. It stands for the harmonious balance and seamless interaction and interconnecting of our spiritual, mental, emotional, and physical realities. It also represents our connection with the natural world. Often called the circle of individual awareness, the Medicine Wheel provides each of us the power over our own lives.

The Royal Alberta Museum describes a medicine wheel to have at least two of these three features:

- A central cairn made of stone

- One or more concentric circles

- Two or more lines extending from the center

Alberta, Canada has nearly 66% of all the medicine wheels of the world. It is the core place for studying medicine wheels. The antiquity of medicine wheels is a matter of debate. Some have been dated as far back as 4000 B.C., the same time as the ancient Great Egyptian Pyramids were built.

But experts have suggested that the Bighorn Medicine Wheel, which is believed to be the oldest and the largest existing one, is millions of years old. Interestingly, medicine wheels were originally called "sacred circles." The phrase "medicine wheel" was coined by immigrants to the North American content in the early 20th century.

The four directions are our advisors and spirits of the world. They establish time and space in our world. The four directions provide a framework for humans to function. They rule our days and seasons. The rising and setting of the sun define our days and give us a way to measure time. The seasons set our annual calendar. During winter, the fields are dormant, preparing themselves for the emergence of new life in spring. Summer is when crops mature, allowing us to harvest them during autumn.

They also provide a strong anchor for our world. Each direction is a lesson for each stage of our lives. When we learn and master the lessons of the four directions, we can master our lives. All issues and problems we face are connected to one or more directions.

Typically, a medicine wheel is divided into four quadrants, one for each of the four directions. Let us look at these directions in detail.

North

North is blue and stands for air, white-skinned people, midnight, stars, death, winter, animals, and the mind or the intellect. The plant associated with the north is sweetgrass. It represents winter and gives a sense of sadness, trouble, and hardships. Winter reflects a season of waiting and surviving and to prepare oneself for the reemergence of life during spring.

Interestingly, the Cherokee word for north translates to cold. The animals of the north are the moose, white buffalo, and bear. All these animals teach us patience, an important virtue for survival.

East

East is red, stands for fire, yellow-skinned people, the sun, and the time of dawn. It represents spring and symbolizes success, power, and victory. Like spring, which emerges with a renewed sense of life, and vigor, East represents growth and development. It reflects the heart or the emotional aspect of people. It is connected to minerals just as the north is connected to animals. The plant it represents is tobacco.

Red also symbolizes protection, which is the reason red beads were used to call upon the red spirit for healing, strengthening love relations, and longevity. Animals of the eastern direction are birds in flight like the hummingbird, owl, and hawk. Chants and sacred words offered to the East help the soul to soar and fly high.

Light a candle for the East because it represents the fire element. It is the direction of new beginnings, new life, births, originality, and creation. The rising sun brings the joy of a new day and a new beginning. Vision is the gift you can receive from the East. Like the sharp-sighted eagle, the power of the East will help you see your world, and you will get insights and the power of discernment. The East guides you on how to live in the moment and be present now. Like spring, it stands for the East in the spring of your soul.

South

South is white and represents water and red-skinned people. It stands for the moon, and the time of day associated with this direction is noon. The south direction is for birth and summer. It is connected to plant life, and the plant this direction stands for is the cedar. Also, the southern direction is for the spiritual aspect of individuals.

Summer is a time for passion, fertility, joy, growth, and peace. The animals of the South are the eagle and wolf. Eagle represents keen eyesight or the power to see everything. The wolf represents the pride associated with belonging to a community or tribe.

West

West is black and represents earth and black-skinned people. The time of day represented by the western direction is dusk. It deals with maturity and the autumn season. Autumn represents the last harvest at the end of a cycle. In the same way, the West represents the end of the summer cycle. West is associated with the physical aspect of life, and it is connected to human life. The plant it stands for is sage.

The animals of the West are the beaver and snake. The beaver is a reminder to prepare for the harsh winter. The snake reminds us we must be ready for transformation just as it sheds its old skin so that a new one can grow.

So, the four directions represent the heart, mind, body, and soul, the four crucial elements of human life. When these four elements are harmoniously balanced, then life becomes a joyful and wholesome experience. Besides the four cardinal directions, there are three more important ones, namely:

- Above - Father Sky
- Below - Mother Earth
- Center - The creator

The Ceremony of the Four Directions

This ceremony is an invocation to the spirits of the four directions. The Shamans of Peru use it to seek the spirits blessings before the start of important endeavors. On a personal level, you can also use this ceremony to seek the blessings of the spirits to help you in your endeavors. Before you start your shamanic ceremonies, you must find your true north.

Finding your true north is an essential aspect of knowing and understanding the power of the cardinal directions. This power helps you understand your stand with the four directions. This knowledge is necessary to connect to the spirit and the natural worlds. Nearly all ancient cultures of the world were in tune and aligned with the stars and cycle of the seasons, which helped them to orient themselves if they got lost. They could use their powerful instincts to identify their location, thanks to repeated practice and being in constant touch with nature.

Keep checking for the true north wherever you are. Set reminders to locate the true north using a compass right through the day. You could check it out at dawn, noon, and sunset. Once you have identified the true north, stand facing that direction, and observe the angle of the sun's rays and other important points (such as the length of the shadow of landmarks in that area). Make mental notes of these observations. This knowledge will be a great guide to help you orient yourself without the help of a compass.

Here is how you can perform this ceremony:

> • First, open a sacred space. You could create an altar for each direction and place them in a circle. Take a deep breath and let go of all thoughts.

> • Align your heart's intention towards the ceremony.

> • Then, face each direction and call upon the spirits by smudging, fanning sage leaves, shaking a rattle, or blowing scented water. Then, say these prayers out loud.

For the South, face the southern direction. Hold one arm up and the other palm open to demonstrate your readiness to receive whatever is given. Repeat this gesture for each of the four directions.

Prayer for the Spirits of the South

The South is vulnerable, sensuous, and playful. It is the direction of emotions and is the best direction to seek help from when you have problems with faith and trust. The South can teach you the importance and power of vulnerability. Praying to the spirits of the south will help you explore the emotions surrounding your vulnerability, so your mind is on high alert, ready to tackle potential problems before they create irreparable damage.

Also, the South is for healing and transformation. Like the snake that sheds its old skin, you will learn to shed oppressive and debilitating ideas and thoughts about yourself and find the courage to accept who you are.

> Salutations to the Great Serpent of the South,
>
> The Winds and Spirits of life-giving water,
>
> Bind and protect me in the warmth of your coil,
>
> Teach me to let go of old ways,
>
> To make a place for the new.
>
> Show me the path of beauty so I may walk my life on it.

Prayer for the Spirits of the West

When you pray to the setting set, you get the power to let go of limiting thoughts and perspectives. The night helps you overcome the pain of the past so you feel reborn when the morning comes. The West is like the cave of a bear, dark and dangerous. Yet, it is where we face our limitations, fears, stale addictions, and patterns alone so we find the courage to get rid of them.

> Salutations to Mother Jaguar of the West,
>
> The Winds and Spirits of the earth,
>
> Teach me and stand by me while I learn to face my fears,
>
> Show me how to transform my fear into love

Show me the way of living a balanced, perfect life,

Let me have no enemies in my life.

Prayer for the Spirits of the North

If you need clear guidance and articulate knowledge and wisdom, then you should turn to the North. It is the mental plane and the home of seekers and teachers of truth. If you are a seeker, then the North will always have answers for you. Winter, the season of the North, is a time of difficulty. It is a period to reflect in silence.

Salutations to the Royal Moose of the North,

The Winds and Spirits of the Air,

Show me the patience for endurance and survival,

Teach me to wait until my time comes,

Teach me to greet you with honor and respect.

Prayer for the Spirits of the East

As you turn towards the East, greet it with respect. Recall the image of the rising sun and the varied colors it drops on the Earth. Ask humbly what gifts and lessons the East can offer you now. Ask the questions you need answers to. Ask for guidance and support. Use the following prayer dedicated to the East.

Salutations to the keen-sighted, high-soaring Eagle of the East,

The Winds and Spirits of fire,

Show me how to soar high and to new places,

Power the wings of my spirit,

Teach men to live with a pure heart.

When you finish the prayers to the four directions, turn your attention downward to the Earth. Touch the earth with one palm and hold the other up towards the sky.

Salutations to you, Mother Earth,

Bless me with healing powers,

Show me the path of wisdom,

Instill in me the power to take care of you so the future generations of humankind,

Continue to revel in your wondrous beauty and abundance.

Next, turn your attention to the sky above, and with both arms raised towards the sky, say the following prayer:

To my father, the Sun, and Mother, the Moon, and the dazzling stars,

Called by a thousand names, I call thy spirits,

And the Supreme Spirit,

Thank you for allowing me to live my life.

Thank you for taking me to the places where I need to be.

When you have finished with the prayers of the four directions along with the three additional sacred ones, namely the stars (which is yellow), earth (which is brown), and the center (which is green), you should close the sacred space. The center is the place of the sacred fire or the self, the center of all life paths.

Set your intention to close the space. You could say your intention out loud or spoken silently in your mind. Thank all the animals and the spirits you have called upon during the ceremony. Then, slowly release the energies back to the four directions. Take a few deep breaths and gradually acknowledge the physical world and the space you are in. Observe any changes in your body, heart, and mind. Be inspired by what you have gained from the ceremony and the sacred space you created. Share this inspirational joy with your loved ones.

While you may use the ceremony and prayers mentioned in this chapter to seek help from the spirits of the directions, as you engage with the process and with each direction, you will find your path, processes, and prayers to do this ceremony. Shamanism believes deeply in rituals, but rituals are not static and are not bound by any rigid structure. Continually changing and updating your ritual processes will help to enhance and renew their powers.

Most important, rituals should be created by the person practicing it. Repeating sacred words borrowed from texts and scriptures will not have the same power when you find your unique way of interacting and communicating with the spirits. The freshness and originality of your processes are excellent to build a deep relationship with your Spirit.

Chapter 5: The Three Shamanic Worlds

There are Three Shamanic Worlds, also called Cosmology. The word Cosmology has its roots in the Greek word cosmos, which means order. Cosmology in Shamanism is identifying the Multiverse. The trick about the Shamanism concept is that it is difficult to translate spiritual ideas into words.

Cosmology and Shamanism

Across various cultures around the globe, cosmology is a study of the universe. Learning Cosmology attempts to try to understand the world. The study specific to the origins of the universe is called cosmogony. The study of the structure of the universe is called cosmology. Learning these two topics may attempt to understand our place in this universe.

According to cosmology in Shamanism, the Sun obtained its fiery headdress from the Primordial Shamans. This fiery headdress powered the Sun to light up the world. In the world of Shamanism, birds are a transformed aspect of the divine Sun, so birds are given a lot of importance by shamans. They are shaman allies and act as mediators between the human and beyond-human realms. Shamans who know the language of birds are endowed with great power.

Cosmological beliefs of other cultures are:

- According to Christianity, a single God created the universe.

- According to Islam, a single God called Allah created the universe.

- According to Hinduism, 330 million gods and goddesses live in a universe beyond space and time, as it is known to humans.

Most traditional cosmologies teach the importance of the circle of life. This means all material and immaterial aspects of the world are not only equal but also interconnected. Everything and everyone is a part of this universal nature. Cultures were awed by what they saw in the world they lived in and revered and respected it. Shamanic practices and rituals enable shamans to access the Upper and Lower Worlds besides the Middle World, which is the Earth we live on.

Shamanism is an ecstatic practice, which means shamans have the power and ability to move beyond the physical, human realm. These flights to and from the different worlds are known by different names, one of which you are already familiar with, namely journeys. Another phrase used to refer to these flights between the realms is "a shamanic voyage." The people of science call it by different names too.

For example, anthropologists refer to shamanic journeys as soul flights. Carl Jung called it "an active imagination." These shamanic journeys take shamans to the lower world, the upper world, parallel physical worlds, and other parts of our world. It takes a lot of persistent practice to know and accept these journeys are not merely active imaginations but allow us to travel beyond our physical bodies' limitations.

Three worlds described in cosmology are the Earth, the sky, and the nether or lower world. Shamans can travel from one cosmic world to another. For example, a shaman can travel from the Earth to the sky and back, from the Earth to the Lower world and back, from the sky to the nether world, etc.

Shamans undertake these journeys to uncover universal mysteries by breaching the limits of various planes of consciousness. The power to communicate with other worlds might seem illogical to the uninitiated, but it is logical because the structure of the universe itself is designed for this interactive communication among the beings of various planes for those with the power to do so.

The Three Shamanic Worlds

In Shamanism, the spirit worlds that shamans visit on their journeys are of three categories, including:

- The Upper World
- The Lower or Underworld
- The Middle World

Shamans travel through the three worlds, often with their power animals or spirit guide, and using a monotonous rhythmic beat of a drum or rattle that takes them into a state of trance. Shamans use an important tool called Axis Mundi or the World Tree. The Axis Mundi is a mythical tree that connects the three worlds. The shamans travel along the trunk of the World Tree to the upper and lower worlds.

Each of the three worlds has its own vibration and atmosphere. Through repeated practice and experience, a shaman learns which world is best suited to visit depending on his or her intention. Different intentions call for journeys to different worlds. To illustrate this point, suppose a shaman needs to seek advice before starting a new project, then he will journey to a spirit helper in the upper world.

The shaman could travel to the lower world to find answers to a different question.

Most shamans travel to the lower world to connect with power animals if they need to heal a sick person, but another shaman seeking a different perspective of the illness could travel to the upper world in search of spirit helpers. As a shaman, the more you practice and learn from your journeys, the more powerful your intuition becomes, which will help you find the right world to find solutions for any problem.

A shaman's interactions with the three worlds also play a big role in his or her choice of the journey. The journeys shamans undertake to the three worlds help them get to know the landscape and the spirit beings better. Let us look at each of the three worlds in detail.

The Lower World

Shamans descend deep underground, the Shamanic Lower World, through the Axis Mundi. The shaman enters a long corridor or tunnel through a portal or opening on the surface of the Earth. This opening could be an animal hole, a small slit at the base of a tree, a small cave at the end of a waterfall, or a staircase that goes into the Earth. The important element is that the opening should be found in the existing world.

Shamanism is deeply connected with transformation and power. The spirit helpers usually take the shape of animals in the underworld. These animals become the power animals of shamans, but spirit helpers also take the form of the wind, trees, guides, and healers too. Although spirit helpers are conspicuously animals, there is no restriction in the form they can take. They can adapt and transform themselves into any shape to share their strength and power with shamans.

These spirit helpers are the key elements to forming a strong foundation of a shaman's practices, rituals, and journeys. They take their shamans to new places in the Lower World. Also, they guide and counsel shamans on their spiritual path. Shamans travel to the Lower World to explore the limitless landscapes there and for transformation and healing purposes. The Lower World also offers power and resources for a shaman's work as a healer and shamanic practitioner for his or her community.

The Middle World

The Shamanic Middle World is the same as the physical world in which we live, but the Shamanic Middle World includes all spiritual dimensions and soul aspects not easily accessible by ordinary humans. So, the Shamanic Middle World goes beyond the real physical world and includes the realms of nature beings, the past and future of the Earth and its inhabitants, and other soul aspects of nature.

Shamans access the Middle World to discover specific information about an event or place on the earth. A shaman journeys to the Middle World to work with or seek help from the soul of a certain being, spirit, or even a natural place. Most ritualistic experiences are based on collaborations between the shaman and the forces of the Middle World.

The Upper World

Located high above the earthly realm, the Upper World is accessed by a shaman when he or she journeys higher and higher in his or her state of trance. Lifted or accompanied by their power animals or spirit helpers, shamans take "the flight of the spirit." They fly to the Upper World empowered by the driving force of the rhythm-driven trance to access the Upper World's spirit helpers.

Shamans can easily experience the transition from the Middle World to the Upper World. Sometimes, the transition is seen as a thin membrane or veil separating the two worlds. Sometimes, shamans who can feel the differences in energy frequencies experience the transition as an alteration in vibration.

The Upper and Lower Worlds vibrate at different frequencies. Also, the spirit helpers of the two worlds are different in how they see things and how they help their shamans. Spirit helpers of the Upper World generally give a higher perspective or a bird's-eye view of things. This perspective helps shamans to distance themselves from difficult situations so they can find the best solution for a problem. Also, the spirit helpers of the Upper World can give you a wider perspective of situations. They can help you discover new and subtle aspects of your being.

Understanding the Axis Mundi

As you already know, as a practicing shaman, you undertake journeys to the three Shamanic Worlds through the Axis Mundi or the Shamanic Tree of Life. This tree is the central axis of the three worlds and runs through the entire Shamanic Cosmos. The Lower World is accessed from the base of the Tree of Life, and the Upper World is accessed from its crown, so the Middle World is on the trunk.

A shaman ready to journey will first focus on the Axis Mundi, the place where he or she gathers strength before their voyage. Here the shaman sets a powerful and clear intention. With continuous practice and help and guidance from the power animals and spirit helpers, a shaman learns to develop an expanding source of power at the base of the Axis Mundi. The shaman can access and experience this power right through the journey.

When the shaman is satisfied with the gathered power, he or she begins the shamanic journey along the trunk of the Axis Mundi. The shaman can travel to the Lower, Middle, and Upper Worlds to meet with and seek help from spirit helpers and power animals.

When shamans are rarely identified through heredity, except among tribes where these customs still prevail in the modern world, so most people's venture into the world of shamanism is through a personal calling or an inexplicable mystical experience. These mystical experiences are often about the person's soul, and often, a spirit animal makes an appearance. If you have had such an experience, then it may be worthwhile to take your calling further and learn about Shamanism and see if you have the mystical power of a shaman inherent in you.

Shamanic practitioners get into a state of trance called "a shamanic state of consciousness" helped by the monotonous beating of a drum or rattle. Entering this state of trance helps shamans access the other worlds. This altered state can range from a light to a deep trance. Highly experienced shamans can even have out-of-body experiences.

Shamans can interact directly with benevolent spirit helpers and other beings of the three Shamanic worlds not accessible to ordinary men and women. Helped by spirit helpers, shamans can diagnose and heal sicknesses. Also, they can seek help and advice from spirit helpers on behalf of other supplicants.

Shamanism is not a matter of belief of faith for shamans and shamanic practitioners. Once you become a shaman and have experienced journeys and have had direct interactions with spirit helpers of the three Shamanic Worlds, then Shamanism becomes as real to you as the sun rising in the east.

As you journey through the three worlds, you discover that compassion, unity, and interconnectedness are the norms in these realms. These ecstatic experiences alter you and your personality, and you realize that you are far, far more than you imagined. Not only that, but you also see that the beauty and magic of the world and the universe you live in are far more than you imagined.

Chapter 6: Shamanic Meditation and Dreams

Meditation is an ancient and one of the most effective ways of turning inwards. Meditation is all about training your mind in ways that will help in inducing a new state of consciousness. Shamanism and meditation are closely interconnected. Shamanism is as much an inward journey to reach subtle spirit worlds as the process of meditation. The effects of both can help you improve your powers of concentration and focus.

Dreams are an important aspect of Shamanism too. Often, the personal calling to become a shaman happens through dreams and the visions seen in dreams. So, this chapter is dedicated to Shamanism's two crucial elements, namely meditation, and dreams.

Guided Meditations

First, know that by meditating, you don't become a different person. You may not even become a better person, especially in the initial days. Meditation is nothing more than training your mind to become more aware of yourself, your emotions, and the world around you. Meditation is about getting a healthy sense of perspective of everything in your life. You learn to observe everything without judgment or bias.

Repeated practice will eventually help you understand yourself, the surrounding people, and the world at large in an improved way.

Meditation is a learned skill. Anyone can learn to meditate and reap its multiple benefits. Meditation is to the mind as physical exercise is to your muscles. The more you work out, the more powerful your muscles become, right? In the same way, the more you meditate, the more you can control your mind.

Starting meditations on your own can be quite a challenge. The most common form of meditation practiced by beginners focuses on the breath. Another important thing to remember about meditation is that it is difficult to perfect. While you are focusing on your breath, there will be numerous occasions when your mind wanders off, and often, you even forget to get your focus back on the breath.

It takes a lot of time and consistent, persistent efforts to learn and master meditation techniques on your own. Having a teacher or guide can help you immensely. This is where guided meditations come into the picture. You can record the following guided meditation notes in your voice. Remember to say the words slowly and softly. Then, play these recordings and do your meditation following the instructions.

Meditation to Find Your Anchor Spot

To reiterate the definition of an anchor spot, it is the place where shamans start their journeys. You can find your anchor spot by using the following guided meditation.

1. Close your eyes and lie down in a quiet, undisturbed place.

2. Take a couple of deep breaths.

3. Count to four as you breathe in (1, 2, 3, 4)

4. Hold for four counts (1, 2, 3, 4)

5. Count to four as you breathe out (1, 2, 3, 4).

6. Hold for four counts (1, 2, 3, 4)

7. Repeat this 4-5 times in your recording so you can breathe deeply during your meditation session.

8. Now, open your third eye or the imagination eye.

9. Now, visualize your anchor spot by answering these questions in your voice:

10. What do you see around you?

11. What scenes do you find delightful?

12. What sounds do you hear?

13. Do you see other beings in your anchor spot?

14. Can you describe your feelings?

Make notes with the answers to the above questions. Then, record your answers so you can play it when you meditate to find your anchor spot. When you have finished, take a couple of deep breaths again, and slowly open your eyes and accustom your senses to your physical surroundings.

Meditation to Find Your Power Animal

Use the same recording as the one you used to find your anchor spot to settle down in this session too. Breathe in and out a couple of times until your body and mind are completely relaxed, and you are ready to make the journey to find your power animal. Then, record this script to continue further.

Imagine a flame emerging from a candle. Visualize your thoughts, ideas, opinions, feelings, prejudices, biases, expectations, and everything else that could change any bias in the ritual. When you are ready to make the journey, the intensity of the flame will reduce slowly and finally go out completely. All your limiting thoughts are now gone with the flame. Take a deep breath in.

Now, imagine a stairway. Visualize it to be made in any way you like. It could narrow, wide, ornate, simple, going straight down, going down in circles, or any other way. You will be going down this stairway into the lower world. Count backward from 10 to 1 slowly. Feel your body and mind relaxing with every step you take in the downward direction. Feel your monkey mind shutting off.

You reach the end of the staircase at the count of 1. You find yourself in front of a beautiful hallway made of the most resplendent glass you have ever seen. The colors and designs of the hallway make you happy and relaxed.

10, 9, 8! You find yourself being drawn deeper into the lower world. 7, 6, 5, 4, 3, 2, 1. You find a door in front of you. Place your hand on the handle of the door and turn it slowly. When the door opens, you find yourself in a little underground cave with a gentle fire at the center of it. The walls of the cave are filled with beautiful crystals that reflect the light from the fire.

You find another door at the end of the cave and walk toward it. You turn the handle and find yourself in a beautiful garden. As you step over the threshold, you see a gatekeeper standing by the side. You ask for permission to enter the beautiful garden you see in front of you. If the gatekeeper allows you to enter, you cross the threshold. Otherwise, you wait there until he permits you to enter.

When you get permission to enter, then walk into the garden and wait at the entrance for your power animal to come to you. While you wait, look at the surroundings and imbibe everything you see. Record your answers to these questions:

- How big is the garden?
- What kind of trees and plants grow there?
- What kind of fruit and flowers can you see?
- What else is unique about the garden in front of you?

When you need to return to the physical world, retrace your steps into the cave, the hallway, and the end of the staircase. Climb the staircase and come out through the portal into your anchor spot. Open your eyes and feel the anchor spot disappear into the Middle World.

Take a couple of deep breaths. Feel your body and mind getting back into the physical world. Allow your thoughts to reenter your mind. Slowly open your eyes. Allow yourself to get accustomed to the real world. Once you record this script in your own voice, play it, meditate, and keep returning to the Lower World until you find your power animal.

Dreams and Shamanism

Interpreting and understanding dreams are important aspects of a shaman's calling. Often, people get the calling to become a shaman through dreams, frequently recurring dreams that simply don't go away and keep appearing as you sleep or rest. So, you should learn more about dreams and how they operate so you can harness their power into your shamanic life.

How to remember your dreams - Dreams are strange, and the scientific community is still trying to understand them and the underlying cause and effects. We remember dreams while others are lost in the wind. When we remember the dreams, they appear and seem real. We don't challenge the weirdness when it is happening and accept it as usual and real.

The thing about dreams is that the weirder they are, the more difficult it is to recall them. The stranger and more bizarre the imagery in your dreams, the worse your ability to recall them. A frustrating element of dreams is that although we cannot remember them, the effects of the dreams, especially nagging feelings and emotions, remain stuck in our minds leaving us worried and anxious without tangible underlying reasons. So, the first aspect of learning about dreams is to know how to remember them. Here are a few pointers that will help you do so.

Science has shown a correlation between the state of mind when we wake up and our memory process, specifically involving neurochemistry processes in our brain. When our noradrenaline levels are high, we tend to forget our dreams, so if we can be careful about the activities that increase the level of noradrenaline, then it will become easier for us to recall our dreams.

The most important element that contributes to elevated levels of noradrenaline is using an alarm clock. When the alarm goes off in the morning, there is a sharp spike in noradrenaline levels, which is a biochemical reaction of our body. Another important reason for spiked noradrenaline levels is sleep deprivation. If you are sleep-deprived, then you tend to fall asleep quickly, which means your brain does not get the chance to experience dreams and store the details in your memory.

Falling asleep is also a biochemical process that takes place in the brain. It shuts down slowly as you fall asleep. Ideally, shutting down the brain takes around 15-20 minutes. If you are sleep deprived, you fall asleep within 15 minutes, leaving no time for your brain to store the dreams you have in your first REM (rapid eye movement) sleep stage, which is when dreams are most likely to occur. Here are a few more tips to remember your dreams better.

Have a regular, consistent sleep schedule - When you are consistent with your sleep and wake-up times, then you tend to have a healthy sleep schedule, so your brain knows when to begin the shutting down process leaving enough time to store your dreams in its memory. Also, a fixed time for going to bed ensures you are not sleep-deprived, which means you will not fall asleep before your brain completes its shutting down process. Also, learn to wake up without an alarm. Both these pointers will significantly improve your ability to recall your dreams.

Have a "shut-down" time - Spend about 15-20 minutes for meditation or relaxation before you fall asleep. This shutdown will allow your brain to catch and store the hypnagogic (the transition time between wakefulness and sleep) dreams.

Don't jump out of bed when you wake up - Take the process of waking up each morning slowly and steadily. It might make sense to drift in and out of sleep for a while. While you drift in and out, try to recall your dreams. This waking up is a habit and will take time to get accustomed to. But once you get the hang of it, you will do it automatically each morning.

Set the intention to remember your dreams each night - Before falling asleep, remind yourself that you want to remember your dreams. As your intention gets deeply ensconced in your mind through repeated reminders every night, your subconscious mind will drive your brain to remember and store your dreams in your memory. While there is no scientific reasoning for this pointer, try it out, and you will notice your ability to remember improves a lot.

Drink three glasses of water before going to sleep - Most often, your body will wake you up to visit the bathroom just after a REM cycle. This is the time you can quickly register your dream in your brain, which is more or less alert when you visit the bathroom.

Don't forget to write down your dreams in the morning - When you wake up in the morning slowly after allowing your mind to drift in and out of the sleepy state, start making notes of your dreams. Write down everything you can remember from your dreams. Initially, it might be a challenging thing to do, but with persistent practice, you can recall and remember your dreams more quickly and more comprehensively than before.

Shamanic Symbols that Appear in Dreams

Symbols seen in dreams and shamanic journeys can give you a lot of insight that will help you in your healing and growth path. Setting an intention to interact with these symbols will make it easy to understand their messages and analyze and interpret their meanings. Here is an interesting story of a shamanic journey that helped a lady understand the symbols that appeared in her dreams better by communicating with them.

For instance, a prospective writer came across a silver spoon while on her shamanic journey seeking help in her writing career, which was not going well. The lady thought that the silver spoon represented her estranged but wealthy parents. She wanted to ignore the symbol because she thought she didn't want to face that aspect of her life. She wanted only a solution for her writing career.

But she changed her mind and challenged the silver spoon and spoke harshly to it through her subconscious mind. She said, "You may be white and silvery right now. But you will tarnish when you encounter the elements of nature." To the lady's surprise, the spoon danced its way with a message she could understand. It told her she had understood the meaning of the symbol well.

That is when it struck her that although she was estranged from her parents and her relationship with them was tarnished by external elements, underneath that tarnish, pure love (like pure, white silver) remained untarnished. When she returned from her shamanic journey, one of the first things she did was reconnect with her parents. This cleared her heart and mind, and she was able to write better, which, in turn, improved her career.

So, even if the symbol you see doesn't seem to align with the purpose of that shamanic journey, you must delve deep and see what the symbol is trying to convey to you. Perhaps, a deeper problem is resolved for a current problem to be addressed effectively.

The trick to learning from the symbols you see in your shamanic journey or dreams is to set the intention to gain insights and learn from whatever is presented to you.

Discovering the Path of Shamanism Through Your Dreams

Often, prospective shamans have many levels of dreams before they finally understand and take on the path of Shamanism. The candidate achieves increasing levels of clarity as he or she progresses through the various stages of dreams. This is a highly interesting and intriguing concept of dreaming in Shamanism.

Shamans who are experts in the field of dreams are called dream shamans. These people tend to be highly experienced and can jump from one dream into deeper levels of the dream. Here's how layered dreaming in Shamanism works.

You go to bed and see your first level of ordinary dreams, which all humans experience routinely. Now, you must consciously tell yourself inside your first dream to go to sleep. That is when you have a second dream which is the second level of a dream. Achieving this second level of dreaming is essential for true Shamanic dreaming.

Again, you consciously tell yourself in your second level of dreaming of going to sleep, which is when you get your third level of dreaming. At this level, you get to see and experience things that are other worldly. The terrain is different. Shamans can speak to and interact with people at the 2nd and 3rd levels of dreaming. They can discover answers to questions.

Like this, it is possible for highly experienced and taught shamans to go into deeper levels of dreaming. It is not an easy thing to do because the soul gets outside of the body and this can get very dangerous. The souls of shamans can get lost in this multi-tiered dreaming experience and getting back these souls requires the power of a specialist dream shamans. For novices, the right thing to do is to take the help of experienced dream shamans and learn your way through the layers of dreams, including how to get back to your physical self.

Thus, dreams and meditation are two vital elements of shamanism you must learn to master to become an effective shaman helping yourself and surrounding people. Both these elements are all about turning inwards into your soul.

Chapter 7: Accessing the Shamanic State of Consciousness

So, how do shamans achieve the altered states of consciousness called a Shamanic State of Consciousness (SSC)? They use different techniques for this, many of which will be discussed in this chapter.

Shamanism is not a religion. It is a practice in which you can connect with beings of the spirit worlds. Shamans are intermediaries between the invisible spirit world and the physical world we live in. Shamanic rituals involve shamanic practitioners or shamans achieving an altered state of consciousness or SSC so they can access the spirit worlds.

Amongst tribes following Shamanism for centuries now, a shaman is a revered individual. He or she is almost always a community leader or doctor. A shaman is believed to be endowed with wisdom and knowledge and has a lot of influence over his or her tribe members. The shaman is also responsible for solving the problems afflicting his or her tribe.

Dr. Michael Harner referred to the altered state of a shaman as a "shamanic state of consciousness." Shamans use different techniques including hypoglycemia, pain stimulation, fasting-driven dehydration, and forced hyper mortality through dancing or moving the body for sustained periods. They also use monotonous sounds and music (discussed in the next chapter), singing and chanting, seclusion, sleep deprivation, and ingestion of hallucinogens, primarily ayahuasca.

Ayahuasca Ceremony

The ayahuasca ceremonies are conducted mostly by Amazonian shamans. Peruvian shamans are known as "Maestro", "Onaya", "Vegetalista", "Curandero", or "Ayahuasquero". Shamans of the Columbian Kofan communities are called "Curacas" or "Taita." Although the shamanic rituals and healing ceremonies vary greatly among the different Amazonian tribes, a common thread runs through them all.

In all the communities, physical and mental illnesses are seen as unresolved disharmony at the spiritual and subtle energy levels. The healing rituals address this disharmony and try to restore the energetic and spiritual balance in the afflicted individual. Therefore, restoration of balance is the ultimate purpose of all shamanic rituals.

In Peru, the shamans conduct the ayahuasca ceremony in traditional round tents called Yurts. The room where the ritual is conducted is considered a sacred space. No footwear is allowed inside the sacred space. Ceremonies are always conducted in groups. Before the start of the actual ceremony and before the medicinal drink is handed over, the members of the group get some time to share their intentions.

Having a clear-cut intention can improve your experience. With a clear intention, you know and accept what you want to let go of in return for help from the spirit of ayahuasca for guidance and healing.

As it is a group ceremony, besides your individual process, you will also have to consider the group process. Thus, the group's energy should be kept intact and should not be broken until the end of the ceremony. Members should not interact with each other during the ceremony, an essential element of respect for the individual and the group processes. The ceremony usually lasts for 4-5 hours.

The shaman leads the ceremony with songs accompanied by musical instruments and smoking sacred tobacco known as Mapacho smoke. Through his or her experience, the leading shaman knows what works best for the group and the individual members. The shaman also knows the right medicine to be given to each member. When the shaman feels the work is completed, then he or she will close the ceremony.

Drinking ayahuasca makes you vulnerable, considering it has psychoactive properties. Therefore, you must participate in ceremonies where you trust the intentions of the shaman, and you feel safe. You must know for sure that the medicine and the group ceremony can facilitate positive transformation within you.

Importance of a shaman in the ayahuasca ceremony - A shaman plays a very important role in an ayahuasca ceremony, and it would be dangerous to participate in one absent a trained and experienced shaman. A shamanic practitioner's primary role is to create and maintain a sacred, secure space in which all the members of the group remain protected from hostile influences of the spirit world.

A shaman's role is not a mere job, but part of his or her life purpose. Traditional shamans are trained for years by experienced shamans from the previous generation. While in training, they are driven hard to face and manage their fears and darkness so they don't pass these unpleasant elements to the supplicants who come to them for help.

The shaman sings a specific song called icaros at the start of the ceremony. These songs are received by the shaman directly from the plants. Participants can easily feel the power of the icaros even if they don't understand the language. The shaman is the channel through which the spirit healers help and heal the sick.

Moreover, every participant's needs are different, and an experienced shaman adapts his or her healing prowess to ensure optimal benefit for each participant and the entire group. A shaman cleanses each group member's energy aura, receives healing power from the spirit helpers, and passes it on to them.

A shaman builds a powerful veil of protection of determination and energy with which he or she can literally "suck out all the negative energies" from all the participating members. However, it is important to mention here that although an ayahuasca ceremony cannot be done without an experienced and powerful shaman, the actual healing power is that of the plant. The shaman is a protective vessel ensuring the entire process happens safely and correctly.

Essential and Popular Shamanic Tools

Shamans need and use multiple tools for shamanic rituals. Let us look at some in this section.

Drum - The monotonous, rhythmic beating of a shaman's drum is like the earth's heartbeat. This tool is deeply entrenched in shamanic practices. Shamans use the drumbeat to journey to the spirit world and return to the physical world with the powers they or their supplicants sought from the spirit helpers.

While the drum and the rattle are essential tools of shamanic practice, they are also allies of the practicing shamans. They have their own soul and power. Traditionally, shamans use handheld drums like tambourines along with a drumstick to beat on them.

So, how do you choose a drum? Where will you find a drum? Which one is best for you? Would it be made of the skin of a particular animal? Is it all right to use a synthetic drum? All these questions can be answered with one sentence – "the most important element while choosing a drum for your shamanic practice is that the sound emanating from it must be pleasing to you, you should be able to dance harmoniously with its beat, and you and the drum should be able to work in sync with each other."

You can work with any drum if the conditions in the previous sentence are fulfilled. Factory-made synthetic drums are less expensive than handmade natural ones. They also have good sound and can be used anywhere outside, even when it rains or is very humid. Many good ones are available in both online and in brick-and-mortar music stores. The crucial thing to remember is that everything, according to Shamanism, has a spirit, even a plastic drum. As a shaman, you must learn to respect it and, in return, the drum or rattles will help you.

Rattles - Rattles not only help the shaman to reach SSC but also act as power antennae. In most traditions, rattles and drums are used together. In Siberia's shamanic tribes, they are built into the drum or are part of the drumstick. Rattles are easy to handle and carry around. They don't bother neighbors, an important element in the modern world when both believers and non-believers live together. Many good, beautifully carved rattles are available at economical rates.

The reason rattles are called power antennae is that many shamans while calling upon their spirit helpers, feel a magnetic power in their hands when using a rattle. The intention is a crucial aspect of any shamanic ritual. When the spirit helpers hear the intention as transmitted by the shaman, they will respond. And if a shaman unwittingly gets lost in the response so much he or she loses track of the intention, then the new intention controls the rattle. Instead of receiving help from the spirit helpers, the rattle gets caught in a power conflict between the power received from the helpers and the new intention. It turns into a battle of powers, and the shaman can feel this experience. This is the reason rattles are called power antennae.

While mass-produced drums and rattles are easily available and work well for shamanic practices, handmade rattles and drums are easily accessible. This is because an increasing number of artisans are creating handmade tools. Several makers hold classes for interested people, and they will teach you how to make your own drum or rattle.

Drumming CDs - Sometimes, using a drumming CD is a great way to start your shamanic journeys. Finding the right drum or rattle, learning how to use it effectively, and other related aspects can take time and energy. For those who cannot buy or work with real drums or rattles, drumming CDs are excellent alternatives. You can play these CDs with your headsets on or use speakers if you are leading a group in a shamanic ritual. It is imperative to treat these CDs with the same respect you would give to the other allies you partner with to contact the spirit world.

Staff - In many cultures, especially in and around Scandinavia, a staff plays an equally important role in shamanic rituals as drums and rattles. The staff, like the rattles, act as power antennae. It is taken by shamans on their journeys and held onto while they travel through the three Shamanic Worlds.

The staff works as a lightning rod. When the staff encounters any change in vibration or power of spirits, it becomes hot and comes alive. It can move like a snake in the hands of a shaman. The staff helps the shaman keep his or her focus on the direction of the path. It also helps to keep the shaman grounded.

Incense - The smoke from burning incense blesses us and spiritually invokes us. Incense can connect with our soul and spirit. Drumming, singing, dancing, and incense smoke together can create a powerful ritual. Burning incense is a sacred ritual designed to gain access to the power of plants and your soul.

When used at the beginning of a ritual, incense smoke helps to define the sacred space for a ritual and opens your soul for the ceremony. Also, incense smoke is used to purify yourself after a ceremony, and your shamanic tools. The purpose of cleansing or purifying using incense smoke is to get rid of negative energies, unwanted spirits, etc., with the power to dent or negatively affect expected outcomes of a ritual.

The herbs used as incense are cedar, juniper, wormwood, sagebrush, woodruff, sweetgrass, the plants of the sage family, etc. While you can buy and use readymade incense available in all stores, you can also make your own incense using the leaves of the plants mentioned above.

Chapter 8: The Power of Sound

This chapter acts as an extension of the previous one. Here, we will discuss the shamanic uses of prayers, mantras, singing, dancing, and playing instruments to achieve an altered state of consciousness.

The Use of Sound, Music, and Song in Shamanism

When languages were still in the evolving stage in ancient cultures, and specifically in oral cultures where sounds played a big role in life, survival was deeply connected to nature. In these communities, sounds helped people to connect their inner feeling with the natural environment. Humans often created onomatopoeic sounds (imitations of cries of birds, animals, and other natural objects and life forms). These imitations were absorbed into shamanic music as well.

Shamans use sounds to recreate an imaginary environment in their minds resulting in a sacred and consecrated space-time in which they made their shamanic journeys and encountered power animals, spirit guides, and helpers. Sounds passed continuously between the inner world of the shamanic journey and the outer world in which the group ritual was taking place involving actions, gestures, and other activities.

In Shamanism, ritualistic sounds were more than simple sounds. They formed a sound system or a symbolic language that helped shamans communicate with their inner and outer worlds. However, the Shamanic sound system was unique in the sense that each shaman created his or her own symbolic language understood only by the creator and those trained by this shaman.

Shamans used a variety of sources to create their sound systems. Each tribe and/or shaman used his or her own unique sound systems. In Siberian shamanism, using hanging metal objects that clanged was an important ritual element. Siberian shamans attached little metallic bells to their ritual costumes and cloaks, to the inside of their drums, and sometimes even to the drum beater.

Consequently, a field of continuously moving sound was created, which was heard as a single, complex sound. Also, shamans used the spatial effects of sound to enhance the ritualistic fervor. They would sing into the drum creating an illusion of the sound was coming from somewhere else. In Mongolia and southern Tuva (now known as Tuvan People's Republic), a jaw harp is known as "khomus", was commonly used to create sound effects in shamanic rituals.

Sounds were also used to prepare the sacred ritual space. Particular types of sounds, especially the sound of bells, are used even today to purify the sacred before the start of a ritual. Purification is a vital aspect of Shamanic rituals as they involve communication with spirits, a potentially dangerous venture. Purification helps to keep negative energies and other pollution elements at bay.

Bell sounds are also used to call upon and send back spirits from and to the spirit world. Shamans also mimic the sounds of animals and birds to call upon spirits. The shamans of the Sami people (an indigenous tribe inhabiting present-day parts of northern Norway, Finland, Sweden, and the Kola Peninsula) have a particular kind of shamanic singing called "Joik", which is about summoning spirits. However, there is a difference between Joik and other forms of summoning spirits with sounds. Joik involves singing about spirits or about representing these spirits. The ritual is conducted on the premise that the spirit is present there and everyone is experiencing the spirit's presence.

Sounds are also used for healing. Shamanism believes in the healing power of sound and music. Sounds are a channel through which spiritual energy is transferred from the shaman to the patient. Among the Tuva tribe, healing sick people using the sounds of a stringed instrument made from the wood of trees struck by lightning is a common treatment.

Shaman's song - A shaman's song is very personal to the shaman. It narrates the story of the shaman and includes details such as his or her birthplace, ancestral pedigree, initiation details, special talents, and special connections with spirits of the spirit world. The shaman creates the lyrics and the melody of shaman songs, and this song remains his or her song right through the shaman's professional career. A shaman's song can be compared to a personal, national anthem.

A shaman's song is called "algysh" in the Tuvan language and is sung somewhere at the start of the ritual. It is invariably accompanied by drumming. As is obvious, the algysh serves as a reminder to the shaman of his or her ancestry, purpose, and identity, which helps to deepen the intention of the ritual. Also, it proclaims the potential visit of the shaman to the spirits.

A shaman's song is popularly called his or her "Power Song." Besides the factual information like ancestry, place of birth, shamanic powers, etc., your power song expresses your nature, individuality, and your true self. Most cultures, like nations, have a power song. And each shaman also has a power song. Power songs are used to prepare rituals and journeying, praying, and healing, for protection and celebration, and more.

The musical notes and the power of your voice as a shaman play a huge part in setting intentions and getting the universal to respond to your intentions. Here is a little exercise that many shamans use with the power of sound and musical notes.

The fourth note Fa in the seven musical notes, namely Do, Re, Mi, Fa, So, La, and Ti is the most important note in Shamanism. Discover this note in your voice. You can use a piano and try to get to the closest approximation in your voice as you strike the Fa note on the instrument.

The Fa musical note represents creation or manifestation. So, if you want to manifest healing, you can send out the intention to the universe upon the musical note. Healing spirits will resonate with your sound of Fa and manifest themselves and their powers to facilitate your intention of healing. Also, the visual symbol for the universe is a square, which represents the power of vibration and thought manifesting into solid, tangible material. Therefore, shamans combine the power of a square with the vibratory sound of Fa. You can also do this.

Find a quiet, undisturbed spot. Close your eyes and imagine a square. Intone the Fa note and observe the square. Notice the image that comes in it. Keep a strong will and intention and put all your emotional energy to create your power song. The stronger your will, the more powerful will be your vibration.

Also, every note on the musical scale stands for a unique vibration pattern in the universe. You can mix and match the notes, although it is best to keep the intonation of Fa as your central note. The personal power song is an important aspect of shamanic healing. You can create lyrics using words, letters, or your own imaginary language. Just remember to keep the base intonation as Fa; the power song will have the right vibratory frequency.

Power songs are almost always used only in private ceremonies and rituals and are rarely sung in public. The only time power songs are sung in public is when a group of shamans engages in combined healing together. And finally, remember your power song is your prayer to the universe.

Shaman's Drum

A shaman's drum typically has these characteristics:

- It is a single-headed frame drum.

- Most often, metallic objects are dangled from a wooden cross-piece inside the drum.

- It is played using a special beater, which could also be the ritualistic rattle

The drum is always made with consecrated materials and is made by a specialist drum maker. The wood for the drum is taken from a tree struck by lightning. The skin for the drum is taken from an animal after careful consideration of various elements. The head of a shaman's drum is frequently decorated with graphics representing the division of the cosmos into the lower, middle, and upper worlds. A shaman more powerful and experienced than the one who will own and use the drum will "enliven" it, which will render spiritual properties to the drum.

Nearly all shamanic rituals begin with the beating of the shaman's drum over a fire. This activity ensures the drum gets tuned to the required pitch. So, why does beating a drum play such an important role in shamanism? Multiple theories have been used to explain this vital phenomenon of shamanic rituals.

One particularly popular theory is called a psychoacoustic effect. The tempo of the drumbeat allows the shaman to achieve a brain wave state aligned with the frequency of the rhythmic beat, which empowers the shaman to achieve an altered state of consciousness. A shaman's portable drum is also highly useful for shamanic rituals replete with gestures and actions.

The physical movement of drum beating is converted into a rhythmic dance. And the tempo of the drum is not always monotonous or regular. It can be slowed down, speeded up, or changed with irregular accents to align with the dance performance. A ritual drum is so personal to a shaman that in some cultures, the skin of the drum is cut after his or her death symbolizing the death of the drum too.

How to Make Your Drum and Rattle

While you can buy a drum and rattle from online and from brick-and-mortar stores for your personal use, you can also make your own at home. Here is a simple method to make a drum of any size, right from a height of a couple of inches to a large, standing drum. You will need these materials and tools to make the drum:

- Rawhide or skin of an animal of your choice. It could be a deer, goat, or any other animal of your choice. You can use the hide of your power animal if you can and want. Make sure the skin is at least 0.75 m to 1.5 mm thick. You will also need a strip of animal skin for the lacing part.

- A wooden hoop – it would be best for you to buy this from the market, considering that it is a complex carpentry task to make it on your own. Make sure it is strong and is at least 300 mm in diameter and 50 mm deep.

- A drum stick

- Water for softening the skin or rawhide

- A couple of cutting and paring tools including a pair of scissors, a knife, and a chisel

The first step is to soften the animal skin. Take a large tub of cold water. Put the skin inside it, ensuring it is completely submerged. It could take a few hours to a couple of days for the skin to soften, depending on the rawhide you are using.

After the skin has become soft and pliable, make markings on it to match the size of the hoop. Ensure the size you mark fits the frame and can be pulled over and held comfortably at the back of the drum.

A key point to remember is to mark on the inner side, which will have cuts and scraped parts, remnants of the places where the skin was removed from the animal during the process of skinning. The outer part of the skin, which looks like leather, will be the visible part, and having marks will give your drum an ungainly look.

Cut the skin along the marking you have made and remember to put it back in the water because you need to keep it soft and pliable to continue your work. You can cut out the remaining part of the skin for lacing.

Next, cut the holes in your drumhead for the lacing to pass through. Cutting holes is best made with a chisel and hammer. Mark the holes correctly before cutting them. Now, pass the lacing through these holes. A vital point to note here is that you cannot stop at this point until you have finished lacing through the drumhead.

When the drumhead is ready, place the hoop over it and lace-up the sides and up the slack. Stretch the lace to ensure it is tight. It works like tying your shoelaces where you place the lace correctly and then pull to tighten it and hold it in place. Only when you create sufficient tension at this stage will the finished product give a powerful, resonating sound. Next, it is time to fix the spokes to tie the drumhead together.

When the drum is finished, allow it to dry. Once it is completely dry, you can paint it however you would like to. You can use a variety of paints to do this. You can also use soft leather to bind the cross at the back of the drum, which will give your drum an attractive profile and cushion your hand from the hardness of the animal skin.

How to make a rattle - Making a rattle is more complex than making a drum. You first need to cut and shape the headpieces of the rattle using soft rawhide. When they are ready, these rattle headpieces should be soaked in a bucket of water until they are pliable. After this, it is time to lace the rattle head. Make sure the lacing work is complete before the rattle head gets hard and unpliable.

Now, it is time to fill the rattle head with sand. Pack it firmly with a stick. Lace the two ends of the free sinews tightly around the neck of the rattle and tie it firmly together. Leave the hanging rattle upside down for a day or two until it is dry.

Now, untie the sinews and pour out all the sand. Fill the rattle head with small stones, corn, or beads, etc. Shake it vigorously to ensure all the remaining sand is removed along with the corn or small stones to empty the rattle head.

Next, assemble the rattle head by filling it with the material that makes the sound you want. Fit the stick into the neck, which will become its handle. Shake the rattle and see if the sound you hear is what you want. If not, add or remove the filling or use any other filling to get the sound of your choice. You can wrap the stick with soft leather to give your rattle an attractive look.

So, you can make your drum and rattle. Yes, it is a complex procedure. For a beginner, it might make sense to buy these shamanic tools from the market. However, as you get deeper into your shamanic role, personalize your drum and rattle, and then, you can make your own.

Chapter 9: The Shamanic Journey

This chapter is dedicated to the most important aspect of Shamanism, namely the shamanic journeys. Let us get right into it.

Understanding Your Shamanic Journey

Shamanic journeys are at the heart of Shamanism. The method of using journeys is one of the primary differences between shamans and other mystics and healers. The journeys are what make shamans cosmic travelers. Only shamans can make their souls travel to other places when in a trance.

According to Shamanism, a part of our soul may leave our bodies and travel everywhere. The soul might leave our body at various times, including while dreaming, to protect us from trauma, etc. Shamans learn to intentionally send their souls on a journey, which is called a shamanic journey or soul flight.

Death is an experience when our entire soul leaves our body. Near-death experiences teach the affected person how to travel with the soul and return. Therefore, in ancient shamanic tribes, nearly all shamans were initiated into the path of shamanism because of a near-death experience they had.

During a soul flight, the traveling soul leaves the body and could travel to any place's spiritual aspect in the cosmos. It could go to places on the surface of the earth (Middle World), go deep into the earth (Lower World), or travel into the upper regions (Upper World). Some cultures have predetermined destinations that shamans visit during their journeys. The Lower, Middle, and Upper Worlds are the most common form of dividing the cosmos. However, there are many more varieties of destinations available for shamans to travel to, depending on the community they belong to.

In Shamanism followed by ancient communities, shamanic journeys comprise three stages, including:

●A period of purification and preparation potentially involving a period of fasting, isolation, and celibacy. Often, a potential candidate goes into the wilderness living by himself or herself during this purification and preparation period.

●The next stage involves finding the power animals and spirit helpers who will help them journey through the three worlds. At this stage, shamanic journeys are usually restricted to the entrances of the three worlds.

●The last stage is when the shaman journeys deeper into the spirit worlds helped by their helpers and guides.

The primary method used by shamans to undertake journeys is by achieving an altered state of consciousness. In this state, a part of the shaman's soul leaves his or her body to travel. The slow, rhythmic beating of the drum or rattle shifts the shaman's rhythm empowering him or her to travel. The drumbeat works similarly to how a soothing song calms frayed nerves.

As a shaman, when you hear the drum's rhythmic sound, your consciousness gets the right state to undertake journeys. The drumbeat frequency is close to that of the earth's rhythmic frequency, which is a vital element for the effectiveness of this method to achieve the altered state of consciousness.

Once the shift in consciousness takes place, then the journey begins. The rest of the journey happens by the shaman's intent. As a shaman, your intention to undertake the journey is the first step. The journey will progress based on your intent. It is difficult to describe how this happens. A perfect analogy for this aspect difficult to put into words is trying to describe how you walk or run. You take the first step, then the second, third, etc., steps follow, right? It happens naturally. A shamanic journey can be similarly understood. You achieve the altered state, and the rest takes place according to the intention of the journey.

Why do shamans undertake journeys? Shamanic journeys work similarly to the way meditation does. It is essentially a tool for spiritual growth. In Shamanism, journeys are also used to heal psychological, physical, emotional, and spiritual problems and get information from the spirit world.

Shamanic journeys allow the traveler to interact and communicate at a spiritual level. Shamanic travelers and journeyers can visit spirit helpers and guardians in the spirit world. While on the journey, shamans can examine and investigate their mental, physical, and spiritual health and that of other supplicants who come to shamans seeking help to overcome problems.

Know there is a difference between a dream and a shamanic journey. In the latter, as a traveler, you have the power to direct your journey as you move forward and learn unexpected things. For instance, if you have a dream of running like a deer, you are likely to feel the speed of the run. In a shamanic journey, you will experience the movement of muscles as the deer runs. If you experience the roar of a lion, you will feel the sound vibrating from the animal's throat.

Even in the world, there are so many experiences that teach you unexpected lessons, right? The same thing happens in shamanic journeys. The more you journey and the deeper you delve into shamanism, the more things you learn, especially unexpected lessons and ideas.

Even if you don't use shamanic journeys to heal others, it is an excellent tool for self-development and building self-awareness. Many followers of shamanism use journeys to overcome emotional issues. During the journey, they meet living or dead people from their lives who have abused or created problems for them.

These journeys provide a safe mechanism to express your angst and anger against such trauma. Consequently, people returning from such shamanic journeys find themselves freed of the trauma's agonizing effects because they have dealt with it in a safe environment, causing no harm to themselves or others. Shamanic journeys, therefore, help people work through their grief.

Shamanic journeys are also seen as a way of growing spiritually. Individuals seek evolved teachers during such travels, and the lessons they learn from these teachers are rife with deep and unexpected meanings that throw light on many dark areas in their lives. Most shamanic travelers report an enhanced level of spiritual attainment as one journey builds onto the next, resulting in seamless and cohesive spiritual education.

You must take detailed notes of all your shamanic journeys on your return. Later, when you read these notes, influenced by newly gained knowledge of each subsequent journey, you will slowly realize the depth of learning you get from each visit to the spirit world. Most messages on shamanic journeys are obtained through symbols, the purport, and interpretation of which take time and repeated journeys to interpret and understand.

The places visited by shamans during their journeys vary depending on many factors, including the intention, the community they belong to, and more. Some places you visit as a shaman will be like what you see on earth. You could see mountains, forests, rivers, valleys, etc. Some other places could be bare and breezy. Some others could give you a deep sense of peace, or you could visit places filled with energy. The destinations of shamanic journeys are not bound by human-bound scientific rules like gravity, etc. Instead, what happens and what is seen is based on the energy of that place.

Some shamans can also journey into smaller dimensions. For example, a shaman can travel to the cells of someone's body to investigate a health problem. Shamanic journeys can also take you to places between molecules of water. Also, some shamans may visit one or two places in all their journeys. Some others could travel to a variety of places during their journeys.

As the shaman gets increasingly skilled at traveling to far-off places and undertaking long journeys, he or she risks not returning. One way to reduce this risk is to have a traveling partner. Typically, this partner would have a keyword or phrase or a particular drumbeat to call the shamanic traveler back to the real world. However, such risky ventures are not for beginners and are meant only for advanced learners who have mastered the basics.

The traveler's experience could also vary on each journey. For example, when you undertake shamanic journeys, you might see everything around you clearly in some travels. In some others, you may not see clearly but can hear well. Some shamans can use all their senses while traveling, while others might only be able to use one of their senses. For example, if the sense of touch is predominant in your travels, you might feel the breeze on your skin or the grass under your feet.

Sometimes, you may experience nothing visual. However, you can sense and interpret messages by merely knowing where you are, and the implicit feeling of knowing something is happening. A good analogy for this seemingly bizarre experience is this. Suppose you are sitting with your back toward the door, and you sense the door opening, and you immediately recognize the person entering before even turning around or hearing the person's voice. This experience has happened to many of us, and many times too, right? A similar experience can be had while on your shamanic journey.

Also, quite often, you can experience the events and happenings taking place in the ritual room and in the destination of the journey. It is like having your soul in two places. The intensity with which shamans experience the events of the ritual room depends on him or her. Sometimes, a shaman tends to cover his or her eyes to minimize the effect of the experiences in the room. As you progress in your shamanic learning, you might master the art so well that it becomes easy for you to block out the experiences of the room, leaving you free to focus on the journey and the messages from it.

The effectiveness of a shamanic journey is measured based on the outcomes. A shamanic healer is considered a good one only when he or she can heal in ways that significantly and tangibly reduce the afflictions of a supplicant. A good shaman can effectively read and interpret the messages he or she receives while on the journey and returns with solutions for the problems on hand. A great shaman returns from the journeys, offering insights using which powerful results can be felt either in the short-term or long-term.

Therefore, regardless of the kind of experience, a shaman has while on his journey, the ultimate test is the outcome and not the experience, which is a personal thing for the shaman. So, if a shaman only hears messages and another sees things in technicolor, it doesn't necessarily mean that the second one is more powerful than the first. The outcome is used to measure the power of a shaman.

The Challenges of Shamanic Journeys

One of the biggest challenges encountered by potential shamans is the lack of trust and taking a critical perspective on shamanic journeys. When you don't trust or are critical of the concept of shamanism, then you get grounded to the earth, and your soul gets tied down, making it exceedingly difficult for your soul to leave your body.

The perfect solution for this challenge is to manage your critical voice and build trust in your capability. Take care of your critical mind before and while on your shamanic journey. You can then use the critical voice to analyze your experiences when you return from your journey. A key point to remember is that new travelers might experience delicate sensations when they return from their initial journeys. However, with repeated practice, their shamanic powers will become increasingly robust provided their critical voice does not crush down their trust.

Interestingly, most expert shamans, especially of contemporary shamanism, believe that a skeptical attitude will not hinder a wholesome shamanic experience provided you don't allow it to interfere with the process. If your critical attitude does not ground you so deeply, your soul finds it difficult to free itself to make the journey.

The mindset is the key differentiator between a shaman who undertakes shamanic journeys and one with a problem lifting off. Keeping an open mind is a vital element in the entire process. Once you have achieved this, then the rest will take place automatically with little or no hitch.

Keeping a closed mind is like closing a door that has immense potential for spiritual growth. You needlessly deny yourself an opportunity for a fulfilling, beautiful experience. And most important, you have nothing to lose. Keep your mind open and get set.

So, the next question for most beginners would be, "Can I undertake journeys?" The answer to this question is a resounding "YES!" An interesting aspect of shamanic journeys is that we all are innately gifted with the ability to undertake journeys. It is a skill we already possess. We only need to be reminded of it. And work effectively to develop and master it so you can achieve higher levels of journeys helped by lessons from each journeying experience.

There is little to teach in terms of undertaking shamanic journeys. Once you get the basic idea behind it and connect with your innate ability, you can find your own ways to develop your natural gift. Often, the less said during the teaching process, the better it will be. This way, learners can delve deep into their minds and psyche and find new paths on their own. Good teachers rarely interfere with a student's innate ability to learn about himself or herself.

You don't have to be a shaman to undertake shamanic journeys. Many novices are effectively using the shamanic journey as a tool for spiritual and personal growth. You may not want to use it to heal or do other jobs that shamans do. You can use it simply for your personal development. Your effort will not be in vain as you notice positive changes in your life.

Chapter 10: The Lower World - Finding Your Spirit Animal

In an earlier chapter, we touched upon the journeys to the three worlds. In this and the following two chapters, we will deal with journeys to these three worlds in detail.

The Journey to the Lower World

Shamans travel to the lower world for the first time, typically to find their spirit animal. Again, this concept was touched upon in an earlier chapter. Here, you will get a more detailed process to journey to the lower world and discover your spirit animal. There are a few important items you will need to make this journey. Here are some pointers to make your journey to the lower world to find your power animal.

First, find a quiet place where you will not be disturbed for at least 20-30 minutes. Be able to lie down comfortably. Have a light blanket. Use a long piece of cloth or bandana to cover your eyes. Have access to an audiotape with a recording, as explained in Chapter 6. You could use a CD with the sound of drumbeats. Keep your journal close by so you can make notes when you return from your journey.

Lie down on the floor and get into a comfortable posture. You can use a pillow under your head or knee for added comfort. Use the light blanket to cover yourself and the bandana to cover your eyes. Turn on the audiotape or drumming CD.

Visualize a place where a special tree grows. It could be a happy memory from your childhood. It could be a tree you, your siblings, and cousins played on. It could be a tree in a special place from your childhood, a place you enjoyed visiting with your family.

Visualize yourself standing in front of this special tree. Observe all the elements on the tree, including its trunk, its branches, the fruit, roots, leaves, the birds that nest there, and everything else you can see. Familiarize yourself with all the aspects of this special tree. Don't be in a rush. Take a few minutes to explore the tree. Wrap your arms around it and hug it. When you are familiar with the tree, then move on to the next step.

Now, get close to the base of the tree, kneel, and look for a hole or a portal through which you can enter the tree. As you persist in your search, you will find this hole.

Next, familiarize yourself with this opening. See how big it is and what things are around it. Keep looking at it and you will notice that the opening which seemed small initially is growing until it is big enough for you to enter with little problem. Now lower yourself down into the earth through this hole. You could visualize yourself holding on to a root as you get down.

As you lower yourself, you will notice the ground beneath you expands into an underground space. Now, this is the beginning of the lower world. Observe the earth as it opens, and rock formations, waterfalls, rivers, streams, fruit-bearing trees, a cave, pool, and other aspects of the earthly life begin to form. Keep following the path until you reach open ground. You are also likely to see the sky and even sunlight.

Experience all the senses, including what you hear, see, and feel. Observe everything happening around you. For example, you could be standing on water because you could feel wet at your feet. You could smell the fragrance of some beautiful flowers growing in a hedge along a forest path. You could hear a bird cooing or the sound of its wings as it flies near you. You could touch the smooth and thorny leaves of a shrub close by.

You could also use your hands to feel your way through the path opening in front of you. Spend some time learning and familiarizing yourself with all elements in the lower world's environment.

Follow the path your senses take you on. If you come across any animal, stop and observe its actions and behaviors. Don't hesitate to ask it if it is your power animal. Typically, if an animal reappears and lingers for some time more than once or twice (while others come and go), it is likely to be your power animal. Here are more pointers to help you identify your power animal:

Recall your dreams - As already discussed in a previous chapter, dreams are deeply connected to our subconscious mind and its memory. So, some things that our conscious mind might have forgotten could be stored in our subconscious mind. These are revealed to us through our dreams. So, recall your dreams and see if a specific animal keeps recurring in them. If there is such an animal, it is likely to be your power animal. If you get to see the same animal in your lower world journey, you can be almost certain that it is your power animal.

Ask yourself if you have an old connection with any animal - Your power animal could be one that was your childhood favorite. It could be a pet you loved, an animal you felt a deep connection with while on a visit to the zoo, or any such past connection with animals.

Write about animals you feel attracted to - Sit down in a quiet, undisturbed spot and get ready to meditate. Close your eyes and take a couple of deep breaths. When you are completely relaxed, think about one animal you feel significantly attracted to. Ask yourself this question, "If this animal that I have special feelings for is my power animal, what lessons can I learn from it? Would these lessons help to build my personal power?" When you get the answers, open your eyes, and write them down in your journal.

Repeat this exercise with different animals and make entries in your journal after each session. Put this out of your mind for a couple of days. Then, return to your journal and see which entry you resonate with the most.

These pointers will come in handy while you are on your lower world journey searching for your power animal. You can quickly identify which animal is your power animal. Before we move on, here is a list of common spirit or power animals that many shamans interact and communicate with:

Butterfly - This beautiful insect is the ultimate symbol of transformation and growth. Its incredible ability to adapt to the most difficult situations and come through with ease and grace is a skill that all of us should learn.

Bear - The bear stands for immense strength. It is a deeply emotional animal and strongly connects with the environment and the earth.

Frog - This animal, which appears to be an unlikely candidate to be a power animal, is an underrated creature. It is the spirit guide of healing both emotional and physical wounds. It reiterates the importance of self-talk and helps heal from past traumas so you can live happily in the present.

Deer - This highly sensitive animal is one of the most powerful intuitive spirit guides. The deer strikes a perfect balance between grace, gentleness, success, and confidence.

Dove - Representing new beginnings, blessings, and peace, the dove is a sign of hope and optimism.

Cat - The cat is a symbol of curiosity, adventure, and independence. The cat is also known for its immense capacity for patience.

Elephant - This majestic animal is a perfect symbol of gentleness, wisdom, and spiritual understanding.

Other power animals that routinely communicate with shamans include the lion, hawk, owl, mouse, turtle, peacock, horse, fox, vulture, wolf, and tiger.

Using the above pointers, you can easily identify your power animal while on your journey to the lower world. Once you have recognized your power animal, find a spot near it, and sit down. Set up a conversation with it. Ask why it chose to be your power animal. Don't worry about your ability to understand the response from the animal. You will sense or even hear its response.

Ask the animal for help regarding any problem you are facing. You could ask your power animal for a little gift to remember the occasion of the first meeting. Keep this gift safe in your pocket. In return, you could leave a small gift for your power animal.

In the first encounter with your power animal, it would make sense to stay with it until you hear your drum's callback clarion. Your power animal is likely to take you on a tour of the lower world. Observe all the places you visit. When the clarion call for your return is heard, thank your power animal, and say goodbye even as you tell it you will return soon.

Now, it is time to make your way back by simply following the path you took in the reverse direction. If you have forgotten the way back, don't worry. Your power animal, which knows the lower world like the back of its hand, will guide you back to the spot where you can climb up and reach the portal at the base of the special tree.

When you reach the tree, slowly bring back the movement in your limbs and gradually open your eyes. When you are completely aware of the physical world, get up slowly. Don't forget to record everything about your journey in your journal.

The most important lesson at this point is that your first journey to the lower world could fail. Failing in the first attempt is a common thing for many shamans. Don't take this failure as the ultimate sign of your inability to undertake shamanic journeys. Remember, the ability to travel is an innate talent all humans possess. We simply need to work on this inherent skill and bring it up to date.

Also, some shamans have only one power animal, which they work with right through their life. However, some shamans have more than one power animal, and they take turns to help the shaman depending on the problem that needs to be resolved. Some shamans have a power animal that is a combination of two.

Working with Your Power Animal

Now that you have a power animal, you must use it by making repeated journeys into the lower world. The more you travel with your power animal, the more powerful you will become as a shaman. Your relationship with your power animal is a vital component of your strength as a shaman. Power animals do not like to be forgotten. Use their special skills to help yourself out of tricky and difficult situations. Don't hesitate to seek its help to help your loved ones too.

All animals have excellent skills for survival. These skills don't help them just to survive but also thrive in the wild. Ask your power animal to share its skills with you so you can use them when you need it. Never forget to thank your power animal for being there for you and for giving you all the help you need.

Also, you mustn't focus only on your power animal's physical aspects. You must identify the spirit of your power animal and learn lessons from it. Your power animal need not show up only when you are on a shamanic journey. You could contact them whenever you want, and they can respond to you in various ways, including through your dreams or visions.

Building a strong relationship with your power animal is a crucial aspect of your shamanic life's success. Learn as much as you can about and from your power animal. Find out:

- What are its physical attributes?

- Where does it live?

- Whether it migrates, and if it does, where does it migrate to?

- What are its mating habits?

- How does it look after its young ones?

- What are its eating habits?

When you have answers to these questions, you might get a sign as to the lessons you need to pick up from your power animal. For example, if your power animal is a bear. You know how much bears love honey. So, it could be a message to you need to have a little more sweetness in your life than your current state. Deeper questions to which you need to find answers about your power animal include:

- How has it been portrayed in ancient stories and myths, and why?

- What are its unique specialties?

The more you know about your power animal, the more you can learn from it and use those lessons for self-development and spiritual growth.

Chapter 11: Answering the Call of the Ancestors

None of us would be here in this world without our ancestors, our closest ones being our parents. Have you tried drawing your family tree? If you have, you would have noticed that the further back we go into our lineage, the more confusing it gets. You may be able to go back about two or three generations, and after that, studying your ancestry can be quite a difficult thing to do. The lines of separation seem to get hazy as numerous sidelines and ancestors emerge in the tree.

If we extrapolated this tree right up to the beginning of humankind, we may all related to each other in some way. Regardless of this interconnection of the entire human race, it is irrefutable that we are the fruit of hundreds and thousands of years of historical lineage and ancestry. There is no doubt that our ancestors have played a crucial part in our existence today. Shamanism accepted and valued the importance of ancestor's way before modern genealogy, and genetic studies demonstrated their value.

Sadly, in many forms of contemporary Shamanism, the concept of ancestry is forgotten as people are increasingly drawn towards spirit guides and power animals. They deserve our respect because we have picked up multiple skills from them genetically. If they had not learned the skills and passed them on to us, we would not have become as technologically advanced and developed today. Each level of our ancestors has passed on certain skills to us. Therefore, we mustn't forget them and must keep them in our hearts and souls.

As a shaman, you will notice it is impossible to forget your ancestors because they creep into your consciousness as you build shamanic skills and practice rituals and journeys regularly. Our ancestors can give us a lot of information about our past considering they were present when the events in the past happened, unlike us who know about these events orally or by reading about them.

You can contact your ancestors living in the twilight area in shamanic journeys and ask for information regarding your own origins. The important thing is traveling to the twilight area where our ancestors live should be done only under the guidance of a highly trained and experienced shaman as the chances of getting lost in these places are high. Interestingly, once you have established contact and a rapport with your ancestors, you can ask them to visit you in your dreams whenever you seek their help.

Shamanic Journey to Visit Ancestors

As with any shamanic journey, you will need two important elements for your journey to meet your ancestors. The first thing is a medium to get you into an altered state of consciousness so you can make the journey and the second thing is your intention. Set your intention by repeating this sentence in your shamanic ritual, "I go to meet my ancestors to seek their help." Your heart and mind should be on your intent, and your deep belief in your ability to do so must be unshakably strong. Don't allow your doubts to mar your ability to undertake the journey to meet with your ancestors.

Also, remember that your ancestors could send you messages in various forms. For example, you could be a traveler where you can clearly see everything happening in your travel and interact directly with your ancestors. However, some shamans hear things and can interpret messages based on what they have heard.

Some others could simply "feel" the answers to the questions. Many of us get our messages from these senses. Remember to trust your intuition and allow the ancestors to connect with you and help you with your problems. Here are some pointers to undertake your journey to the shamanic world to meet your ancestors. Let us begin.

Find a quiet, undisturbed spot and lie down comfortably with a light blanket covering your body and a bandana or a piece of cloth covering your eyes. Turn on the CD of drum beats or any form of recorded audio you use to get into an altered state of consciousness.

Relax your body and mind slowly and steadily as you listen to the drumbeat in the background. As you relax completely, state your intention to visit your ancestors a few times.

Imagine you are in a vast meadow standing near a wall. Explore your surroundings. Observe the green grass, the sheep and other cattle grazing peacefully nearby. Watch everything closely and familiarize yourself with your surroundings.

Slowly but as your intention gets deeply embedded in your psyche, you will notice a door in the middle of the wall. Walk slowly to the door, turn the handle, and open it. Step over the threshold and stand there. While you wait at the entrance of the grove, build up a deep sense of anticipation of meeting with your ancestors.

You see a large grove on the other side of the wall. It is filled with beautiful green trees. A lot of luscious, juicy fruit is hanging from many trees. There are rows and rows of them. You see birds and animals moving around peacefully in the grove. Listen to the sounds of birds and animals, the gentle breeze, a flowing brook, etc. Feel the ground beneath your feet. Thank the spirits of the four directions in your mind.

Look for signs in the grove that seem to beckon you. It could be a light coming from deep within the grove. It could be a voice you recognize (your parents or grandparents) calling you over to meet them, or any other similar sign. Keep all your senses alert to read and interpret these signs.

Trust your intuition and walk toward the sign you sense as a calling from your ancestor. Find an inviting spot and sit down in the place that the sign leads you to. Again, look at the surroundings and familiarize yourself with them using all your senses, including sights, smells, touch, sounds, and feelings.

Call upon your ancestors to come and join you at your waiting place. Speak your intention of calling upon your ancestors to come and visit you a few times. "I want my ancestors to come and visit me here."

Shortly, you will experience the presence of someone standing close by waiting for your cue to invite them to join you. Look at the person and see who has chosen to visit you. How many of your ancestors have come to see you? One? Two? Three? Many? Are they male or female? Be open to all options and simply accept whoever you visit. Trust your ancestors to send you the right kind of people to help you.

Thank and honor your ancestors by saying, "I thank you for accepting my invitation to meet me. I honor you. I thank you for giving me life." Repeat these sentences until you are satisfied that your ancestors have the message and appreciate your feelings toward them.

Now, simply allow things and events to unfold on their own. Your ancestors might talk to you, or you could simply sit in companionable silence with them. While you can interact with them, it would be best for you to simply observe them and give them the right of way. Let them lead you to wherever and whatever they believe will help to you.

You could ask a specific question. However, be patient and wait for them to respond at the appropriate time. The trick is to be patient and wait for things to happen at their natural pace and time. You might have to sit with your ancestors for a while. In fact, during your first journey, you might or might not get the answers and help you seek.

You might have to return when you hear the callback sound and make another journey another. The spirits of our ancestors also work similarly to the power animals. They take time to build a rapport with you. Just remember that once you have connected with them on your first journey, they will contact you through other means, including dreams, visions, etc.

The thing to remember is not to be frustrated with seeming failure in your attempt to connect with your ancestors. It takes time and diligent effort. They will come when the time is right. Keep your intent strong, and they cannot and will not ignore you. A part of them is embedded in your DNA, and they live in a world that has no restrictive physical boundaries. Just sit with your ancestors until the callback sound is heard. Accept whatever happens during your time with them.

When you get the callback sound, allow your ancestors to fade away. But before that, you must remember to thank them for their time. Show your profuse gratitude by saying, "I thank you from the bottom of my heart for seeing me. I honor your presence in my life."

Also, let them know if you will see them in any form. Permit them to send you messages as they deem fit. Let them know you will visit them again soon. Our ancestors love having visitors because few people visit them, considering that making journeys takes time, effort, and diligent practice. So, assure them you will return soon. After they have faded away, walk back to the physical world through the entrance you came in. When the drumbeat stops, slowly bring movement into your hands and legs. Open your eyes, get accustomed to the real world, and get up gradually. Make detailed entries into your journal.

Shamans and Their Ancestors

Once shamans make contact and build a rapport with their ancestors, the relationship can get deep. Shamans get summoned by specific ancestor shamans to do their bidding. In some cultures, like the Tungusic tribes, shamans get afflicted with an inexplicable form of fits or illness, which could be a sign of the summons of an ancestor shaman.

Ancestors of other tribes use more humane methods to summon shamans. They could use dreams or visions to send shamans messages. For example, shamans of the Zulu tribe get visions and dreams from their ancestors. The ancestors of the Blackfeet tribes in North America leave signs in nature for shamans to read and respond to the summons.

Sometimes, especially when a shaman has not attempted to connect with his or her ancestors, the summons could come through the power animal or spirit helper. These calls from ancestor shamans are invariably to initiate the chosen person into shamanism. Ancestors see potential in a chosen candidate and wish to initiate him or her into the path of shamanism.

Once initiated, the ancestors continue to offer help to the new shaman in all journeys and healing rituals. In some cultures, a shaman's primary helper could be an ancestor instead of a power animal or spirit helper. Hmong shamans have a group of spirit helpers and power animals led by an ancestor who is called the Ancestor-Master. This Ancestor-Master bequeaths the power of his human spirit to the descendants of the tribe so they can carry on the work he or she started. The ancestor spirit continues to help his or her descendants.

Ancestor spirits also help shamans conduct many rituals. In certain tribes, shamans call upon their ancestors to help them out when tested for their skills before being inducted as shamans of the tribe. The response of the ancestor is a sign of the candidate's shamanic powers.

Among the Mongolian tribes, when a shaman is possessed during a shamanic ritual, he or she is considered possessed by "grandfather" or "grandmother", which is highly symbolic of ancestors.

Undoubtedly, ancestors play a crucial role in Shamanism, specifically in an individual's success as a shaman. It would, therefore, be naive not to acknowledge the wisdom and power of our ancestors. Instead, we should harness the power they are almost always ready to give to their descendants.

So, remember to connect with your ancestors. Discover more about your ancestors and see which one of them you would like to build a rapport with. When your ancestors hear or sense your deep intention to connect with them, they will never hesitate to contact you and help you in every way you need.

Chapter 12: The Upper World - Encountering the Divine

This final chapter will look at the Upper World journey and see what experiences you can have as a shamanic traveler. So, let's get straight to it. Shamans travel to the Upper World to obtain archetypal wisdom, get a higher perspective of their own lives or those of their supplicants, or influence the leaders to make better choices for their tribe's overall goodness of their tribe.

Shamans also visit the Upper World for insight and inspiration to be able to restore balance in their community. Maintaining balance and harmony is a key responsibility of a shaman. The good thing about journeys is that they can be undertaken by anyone right from the novice in the world of Shamanism to the most experienced shaman. It takes a bit of imagination and a powerful intention to seek help and find answers to your various questions.

The Upper World is as magical as the Lower and Middle Worlds of the Shamanic cosmos. Here, you can meet and connect with your celestial parents, who can help you access and understand your original soul agreement, the ultimate guide to your life purpose.

One small piece of advice as you start your upper world journey is that you are likely to be overwhelmed by the power this part of the cosmos holds. It is also likely that in your excited frame of mind, you could ask a million questions. Remind yourself to take things slowly and to hold back your excitement. Revel in it. However, remind yourself that you will be making these trips to the Upper World repeatedly. There will be plenty of time for all your questions.

It is best to travel to the Upper World with your power animal as your guide. Your spirit animal's powerful instincts and survival qualities are excellent tools of guidance. It is your perfect companion to flight to your Destiny. The Upper World's power animal can be similar to the one you obtained for the Lower World. However, typically there is a small difference.

The upper world's power animal is almost always a creature that can fly like the hawk, eagle, or dove. These winged creatures are perfect for giving you a bird's eye view of the cosmos, which will help you immensely to put your own life into perspective. As with all shamanic journeys, it makes sense to record your experiences on your return. As before, record your voice with the following script so you can play it when you start your journey to the upper world.

Sit on a comfortable chair, or better still, use a recliner. Take a couple of deep breaths before starting. Close your eyes and place your hands on your lap. Allow your body and mind to relax, ensuring you are fully engaged in the present moment.

You can use this breathing exercise to relax before the journey. Inhale to the count of seven, hold for a count of seven, exhale for a count of seven or more until you feel your lungs are completely out of air. Repeat this process a couple of times, which will help you feel relaxed, although, in the initial stages, the count of seven, especially during exhalation, might be a challenge. However, with a bit of practice, you will be able to get the hang of it easily. Also, you can use this breathing technique for your journeys to the Lower and Middle Worlds.

When you are completely relaxed, state your intention to travel to the upper world. Say these intentions out loud:

> • I would like to travel to the Upper World and meet my celestial parents.

> • I want to journey to the Upper World (state your purpose).

When I journey, I want to be contacted only by pure beings and by light. These restrictions include my ego and any other limiting thoughts I might have.

Repeat this intention often until you are satisfied that it has reached the spirit helpers.

Now, imagine a tall, gigantic tree in front of you. This tree is your Axis Mundi through which you will be climbing to the Upper World. Visualize its huge and spacious trunk, its large roots holding the tree strong and steady, a labyrinth of branches extending into the sky above. Imagine yourself getting into the spacious trunk of the trees. Think of yourself being inside it.

Visualize the sap of the tree flowing from the root toward the top of the tree. Allow this thick flow of sap to carry you up into the higher branches until you reach the topmost branch. You will reach a place above the clouds. Here is an important point to remember. You are free to imagine any kind of scene to make your journey. Just to remind you, you start your journeys from your anchor spot. Here, the gigantic tree was the anchor spot.

You could use the same anchor spot you chose for yourself when you visualized it for the first time, as described in chapter 3. Here is another way your visualization powers will take you up to the heavens. When you feel relaxed after the breathing techniques, you can visualize a large, green meadow.

When you reach the area above the clouds, look around you and familiarize yourself with the place in the heavens. Find a solid cloud on which you can stand and float around in the Upper World. Now, call out for the gatekeeper. Like the Lower World, the Upper World also has a gatekeeper, and you need his permission to enter. Observe the gatekeeper walking towards you.

When he gets close, tell him your intention for your visit to the Upper World. He will permit you to walk with him into the Upper World. As you walk alongside the gatekeeper, look at the surroundings, and take in the beauty of the scene in front of you. In some shamanic cultures, there are multiple levels in the Upper World. The gatekeeper will take you level by level and show you around.

In the first level of the Upper World, you will see a cave-like room filled with many minerals and crystals. Absorb everything you see there. You will soon notice a small path ahead of you right in the middle of rows and rows of minerals and crystals laid out in all their splendor in the cave room.

Take this path until you reach a doorway. Turn the handle and open the door. You will see a desert-like atmosphere. Notice the spiral staircase that opens in front of you. Climb up the stairway feeling the warmth of the desert sun drenching you in sweat. You will find a wall with a small gap for one person to walk through at the end of the stairs.

Walk through the gap into the shade of a beautiful grove filled with fruiting trees and numerous rows of flowering plants. You will notice that the gatekeeper is right beside you. He will lead you to a waterfall and ask you to walk through the soothing waters. You do as he tells you and get under the waterfall. You will notice the warm water soothing and relaxing you after the long, long walk to the grove. This is part of the cleansing preparation before you can meet your celestial parents.

When you feel ready, request the gatekeeper to call for your celestial parents. You will notice two bright lights coming toward you from a distance. As these lights come close to you, greet them respectfully. Thank them for coming to see you. Sense the love and affection they feel for you and allow the warmth of this love to pervade your entire being. You can begin talking with these spiritual beings by asking these questions:

- Who are you?

- Are you my celestial parents?

- What is your relationship with me?

As you ask these questions, you will notice that their thoughts and yours combine and become one thought. So, you ask the question, and the answer is also in your head because of the thoughts becoming one. You will realize there is no separation or limiting boundaries between you and your celestial parents. You experience everything they do, and because of this seamless connection with your celestial parents, you can perceive and experience each other's thoughts and feelings. Spend some time with your celestial parents exploring the Upper World.

After building a good rapport with your celestial parents, seek their help in recalling the original sacred contract formed between you and the universal spirit before you made an entry into this lifetime. Ask them questions related to your life, such as:

- What made you choose your biological parents?

- Where were you born?

- What are the circumstances surrounding your birth?

- What are the experiences you wanted to have when you choose this lifetime?

- Have you been true to the terms of the contract? If no, where and how much have you deviated from the original path? How can you correct your course?

All these answers will be found in the original sacred contract. Remember, don't ask all these questions on your first encounter with your celestial parents. These are questions they can answer, and which will help you improve your self-awareness and make a better and more meaningful life than before.

This interaction with your celestial parents will help you understand the core purpose of your life. Now that you have lived your life on earth and have new experiences to add, you can renew your contract with new clauses aligned with what you want to do in this lifetime.

Let your celestial parents know about your new plans. Let them know how you plan to learn, love, and experience more of your life than you are doing right now. Sharing your goals with your celestial parents will drive commitment in you because you know they will follow up with you to ensure you keep your promises made to yourself.

Ask your celestial parents to take you to the place where your ancestors live. You can visit them for a while and get to know them well. When you have finished your work in the Upper World, thank your celestial parents again and begin your journey to return to the physical world. Don't forget to thank the gatekeeper before you begin your journey down the special tree, the Axis Mundi.

Now, call upon your winged power animal to take you back to the physical world. Feel the wind blowing against your face as your power animal carries you to the base of the Axis Mundi. When you have reached the base of the tree, thank your power animal for getting you back safely. Slowly, return to your body and open your eyes. Move your hands and legs to get back your mobility in the physical world.

Return to your world with all the wisdom you gained from the Upper World, especially from your celestial parents. Don't forget to make detailed entries in your journal. When you return from your journey to the Upper World after meeting your celestial parents, you will feel a profound sense of accomplishment and happiness.

The opportunity to realign your life with your true purpose will energize and rejuvenate you readying you to meet life's challenges. The connection with the celestial parents is permanent. Once you've made it in this world, you cannot disconnect from them even if you want to. They will appear before you at the slightest hint of trouble. Their added guidance will help you deal with life's problems in a much better way than before. They will be there to welcome you back to the celestial world when you finish your life purpose in this lifetime.

Your perspective from the Upper World will differ greatly from that which you experience in the Lower or Middle Worlds. From here, you can see everything in your life as one cohesive unit. You see your life and individual life events from a more mature perspective than before, empowering you to make positive changes in your lifestyle.

Conclusion

In this concluding note, summarize key lessons from this book.

Shamanism is not just an ancient healing system but a way of life. By building and leading a shamanic way of life, you can lead a more meaningful and happy life than before. You will feel the interconnectedness of the entire cosmos as you increase your experience with shamanism.

The medicine wheel is an important aspect of shamanism as it helps you understand the value of the four directions and teaches you how to seek help from the spirits of these directions.

Experiencing the cosmos' non-ordinary realities and traveling to the Three Shamanic Worlds requires you to achieve an altered state of consciousness. This state can be achieved in various ways, including listening to a repeated, monotonous drumbeat, using ayahuasca, alcohol, and certain smoke.

However, it is vitally important not to try to get into altered states of consciousness using alcohol or other forms of substances on your own. You must take the help of an experienced and trained shaman to do so. Doing it with half-baked knowledge can prove highly dangerous. The drumbeat is the safest, and with a little practice, can be an effective method of achieving a shamanic state of consciousness.

Sounds, meditation, and dreams play an important part in Shamanism. Messages from spirit guides come in the form of signs, visions, and dreams. However, sometimes, shamans can directly interact and communicate with spirit helpers, power animals, and ancestors.

Now that you have completed one reading of the book go back and reread each chapter more slowly than before. Follow the instructions in each chapter and perform all the activities mentioned in it. The more you learn about yourself in Shamanism, the more empowered you become.

Here's another book by Mari Silva that you might like

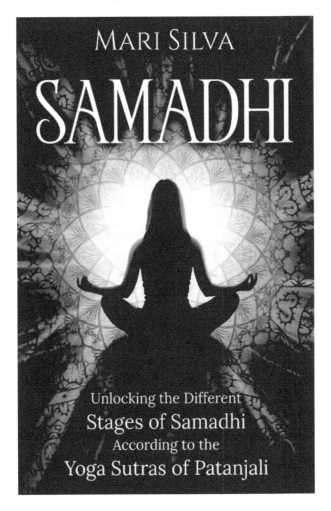

Your Free Gift (only available for a limited time)

Thanks for getting this book! If you want to learn more about various spirituality topics, then join Mari Silva's community and get a free guided meditation MP3 for awakening your third eye. This guided meditation mp3 is designed to open and strengthen ones third eye so you can experience a higher state of consciousness. Simply visit the link below the image to get started.

https://spiritualityspot.com/meditation

References

6 Steps to Help You Remember Your Dreams. (n.d.). Psychology Today. https://www.psychologytoday.com/us/blog/sleep-newzzz/201907/6-steps-help-you-remember-your-dreams

An Encyclopedia of Shamanism, Volume One: A-M: Pratt, Christina: 9781404211407

Bock, N. (2005). SHAMANIC TECHNIQUES: THEIR USE AND EFFECTIVENESS IN THE PRACTICE OF PSYCHOTHERAPY. https://core.ac.uk/download/pdf/5066663.pdf

Dobkin de Rios, M. (2002). What We Can Learn From Shamanic Healing: Brief Psychotherapy With Latino Immigrant Clients. American Journal of Public Health, 92(10), 1576–1581. https://www.ncbi.nlm.nih.gov/pmc/articles/PMC1447282/

Drake, M. (2012, March 29). Shamanic Drumming: Crafting a Shamanic Drum. Shamanic Drumming. https://shamanicdrumming.blogspot.com/2012/03/crafting-shamanic-drum.html

Gaia - Conscious Media, Streaming Yoga Videos & More. (n.d.). Gaia. Retrieved from https://www.gaia.com

Gates, D. (2011, May 31). 13 levels of shamanic dreaming. Dream Gates. https://www.beliefnet.com/columnists/dreamgates/2011/05/13-levels-of-shamanic-dreaming-2.html

Home. (2018, July 24). https://www.roelcrabbe.com/

How a Shaman Rattle is Made. (n.d.). Www.Beardrum.com.
https://www.beardrum.com/rattleconstruction.html

Joseph, B. (n.d.). What is an Indigenous medicine wheel? Www.Ictinc.Ca.
https://www.ictinc.ca/blog/what-is-an-indigenous-medicine-wheel

Journey to the Four Directions - Pointers in Sacred and Shamanic Work. (n.d.).
Byregion.Byregion.net.
https://byregion.byregion.net/articles-healers/Shaman-Directions.html

—Journey to the Upper World. (2020, May 19). The Four Winds.
https://thefourwinds.com/blog/shamanism/journey-upper-world/

Lower World Journey. (n.d.). Journeys To The Soul.
https://journeystothesoul.com/shamanic-journeys/lower-world-journey/

Mircea Eliade, & Vilmos DiÃ³szegi. (2017). Shamanism | religion. In Encyclopædia
Britannica.
https://www.britannica.com/topic/shamanism

Monahan, J. B. (2018, August 7). Working with Your Power Animal. Medium.
https://medium.com/@jennifermonahan_28426/working-with-your-power-animal-a5d4cdf00e5a

PhD, D. K. (2019). Dances with Ancestors: The Shaman's Guide to Engaging the
Old Ones. In Google Books. iUniverse.
https://books.google.ro/books?id=JMzBDwAAQBAJ&lpg=PT23&ots=zVb06b4TT
Y&dq=shaman%20ancestors&pg=PT5#v=onepage&q=shaman%20ancestors&f=false

Power Songs: Where Do I Get Mine? by Shaman Elder Maggie Wahls / Shaman
Portal. (n.d.). Shamanportal.org.
http://shamanportal.org/article_details.php?id=535

Shamanic Tools - Drums, Rattles, Flutes, Staffs, Incense. (n.d.).
Www.Shamanism.Dk.
http://www.shamanism.dk/tools.htm

Shaman's Way - Shamanic resources including articles, podcasts, free drumming
music and more about shamanism. (n.d.). Shaman's Way. Retrieved from
https://shamansway.net/

The Shamanic Journey. (n.d.). Shaman Links. https://www.shamanlinks.net/shaman-info/about-shamanism/the-shamanic-journey/

The Shamanic Journey: Experiences, Origins, and Analogues. (n.d.).
https://drrogerwalsh.com/wp-content/uploads/2011/02/The-shamanic-Journey-Experiences-Origins-and-Analogues.pdf

The Shamanic Offering. (n.d.). http://www.kondor.de/. https://www.kondor.de/shaman/ancestors.html

What Is a Shaman and Can Anyone Become One? (2020, May 27). HowStuffWorks.

https://people.howstuffworks.com/shaman.htm

What is a shamanic ayahuasca ceremony and why work with a shaman? (n.d.). Acsauhaya.

https://acsauhaya.org/shamanic-ayahuasca-ceremony/

Made in United States
Orlando, FL
12 November 2024

53801241R00068